# Legal Positivism, Politics, and Critical Ethics

# Legal Positivism, Politics, and Critical Ethics

Elena Namli

BLOOMSBURY ACADEMIC
NEW YORK • LONDON • OXFORD • NEW DELHI • SYDNEY

BLOOMSBURY ACADEMIC
Bloomsbury Publishing Inc, 1385 Broadway, New York, NY 10018, USA
Bloomsbury Publishing Plc, 50 Bedford Square, London, WC1B 3DP, UK
Bloomsbury Publishing Ireland, 29 Earlsfort Terrace, Dublin 2, D02 AY28, Ireland



First published in the United States of America 2025



A catalogue record for this book is available from the British Library.

A catalog record for this book is available from the Library of Congress

ISBN: HB: 978-1-6669-7340-2
ePDF: 979-8-7651-9293-1
eBook: 978-1-9787-4935-1

Typeset by Deanta Global Publishing Services, Chennai, India

*To Carl-Henric Grenholm*

# Contents

Acknowledgments ix

1 Introduction: Law, Morality, and Politics 1

2 Beyond Natural Law 29

3 H. L. A. Hart: Utilitarian Ethics and Democratic Law 49

4 Joseph Raz: The Legitimate Authority of the Law and Political Morality 73

5 Jürgen Habermas: Democracy and the Law 97

6 Legal Positivism, Democracy, and Moral Critique of Law 123

Bibliography 153

Index 159

About the Author 163

# Acknowledgments

I would like to express my gratitude to those individuals and institutions that in various ways have supported the research project which has resulted in this book.

Over the six years I have been working on the book, many others have helped me. I am grateful to all members of the research seminar in ethics at the faculty of theology at Uppsala University. Special mention must be made of Carl-Henric Grenholm and Per Sundman, who kept supporting and challenging me through several versions of the manuscript.

I am deeply grateful to Mark Klamberg, Lars Lindblom, Patricia Mindus, Johanna Romare, Torben Spaak, and Mikael Spång for their most generous comments and critiques of my project.

I have benefited from excellent comments and suggestions from many friends and colleagues in *Societas Ethica* for which I have had the privilege to serve as a president.

The *Olaus Petri Foundation* at Uppsala University has provided financial support for the most valuable workshop on the first draft of the manuscript at *Sigtuna Foundation* in April 2023.

I owe my students at the master's program in human rights huge gratitude for their great questions and, most importantly, all the energy they invested in thinking and taking human rights seriously.

Uppsala, October 2024

# Chapter 1

# Introduction

## *Law, Morality, and Politics*

Modern law is one of the most important institutions in a democracy, perhaps the most important. Power—political as well as economic and discursive—is exercised under the law. Simultaneously, modern law is a result of the exercise of power, which means that in a democracy, the subjects of the law are considered to be authors of the law. For those who, for different reasons, act in order to transform or even replace democratic orders, the law can be both a hindrance and an instrument of their efforts.

Although we can easily agree that the quality of the law is decisive for the future of democracy, we reasonably disagree about the very meaning of good law. These disagreements concern several dimensions of legal regulations—from institutional efficiency to morality. This book will deal with the latter.

Under what conditions is the law morally justified? Let us start with an example. Legally protected human rights, that is, legitimate claims on behalf of each and every person toward the state, are a revolutionary element of modern law and democratic politics. In a clear break with the historically dominant view that the state is authorized to demand obedience and impose duties on citizens, human rights legislation imposes obligations upon states. Individuals as well as minorities are granted rights that the state is obliged to respect. Violations of these rights constitute an exercise of illegitimate power by the state.

In a democracy, human rights legislation is justified by the idea that citizens are the source of legitimacy of power exercise and the state is instrumental in relation to this power.

Now, let us consider a situation in which influential political agents in a democracy act in order to reverse this development. Their aim is to strengthen the power of the state and to weaken the rights of individuals and minorities. Law is the most important target of such a project. One frequently used strategy is the reinterpretation of human rights in a way that transforms them from being a constitutional framework for the legitimate exercise of state power into moral values that individuals are required to embrace. Antidiscrimination laws that represent a genuine human rights culture are now put under suspicion while legislative initiatives that promote assimilation or/and exclusion of minorities are framed as a defense of human rights.

Islamophobic misrepresentations of Islam and Muslims in contemporary Europe, for example, take the form of "protection" of human rights and democracy. Islam is incompatible with human rights, it is claimed. Moreover, Islam's morality and law are depicted as a direct threat to the legal and political culture of Europe. Thus, Muslims and other minorities are expected and sometimes even forced to accept certain "democratic" moral principles and values that are claimed to be shared in common by a society. Representatives of the state are encouraged to regard themselves as guardians of civic morality rather than as acting in accordance with laws that protect individuals and minorities from power abuse and discrimination on behalf of the state.

Whenever such a development takes place, our moral and political responsibilities as democratic citizens require us to act. But what should we do and what do we need to know about the law in order to protect democracy and justice? Under what conditions is the law morally justified? From what perspective should a reasonable moral critique of law be framed?

The purpose of this study is to develop a theory of the relationship between law, morality, and politics that answers these questions. This theory recognizes the positivity of modern law as its fundamental feature—that is, views legal regulations as products of political activity of legislation[1]—and simultaneously offers instruments for a moral critique of law. To analyze modern law in such a way means in practice to construct a theory of the relationship between law, morality, and politics.

In this study, I therefore assume that in order to develop a theory of modern law that recognizes its positivity and endorses the demand for a moral critique of posited regulations, it is not enough to account for the criteria of legal validity. We need to combine a plausible account of legal validity with a plausible approach to moral justification and an understanding of the relationship between morality and politics. Accordingly, the theory we seek must fulfill three conditions. First, our theory should give a reasonable account of the legal validity of social regulations. Second, our theory should encompass the criteria for morally justified law. Finally, our theory should offer a reasonable understanding of democracy as the arena where law, morality, and politics interact.

The theory I will defend and develop in this book is related to, and should be understood in the light of, earlier philosophical discussions of the relationship between law and morality. These discussions used to be framed either a defense of natural law theory or a variation of legal positivism. Let us therefore recall the most important elements of the controversy between natural law and legal positivism.

## THE DIALECTICS OF LAW, MORALITY, AND POLITICS

Under which conditions are posited legal regulations valid? This question has been and still is central to philosophical discussion of the relationship between law and morality. Should the criteria of legal validity necessarily include moral demands? In the European context, proponents of natural law used to be the most vocal defenders of the thesis that the moral quality of legal regulations is a necessary condition for the proper functioning of the law. The natural law tradition thus regards the moral quality of the law as a component of its validity.

Legal positivism rejects this thesis, claiming that there is no necessary connection between the validity of legal regulations on one hand and the moral quality of such regulations on the other. Valid law and morally justified law are separate concepts and, in the wording of Herbert Hart, "it is in no sense a necessary truth that laws reproduce or satisfy certain demands of morality."[2] This "separation thesis" unites legal positivists of different schools.

Various forms of natural law theory—theological as well as secular—gained new energy after the Second World War. A broadly accepted explanation of this dynamic is that many theorists and practitioners of law and democracy saw developments in Nazi Germany as being related to the embracing of legal positivism by influential German lawyers and legal scholars. Thus, the revival of natural law was in many regards an attempt to counteract a legal positivism that in Nazi Germany had legitimized profoundly immoral legal regulations. Such a legitimization was not a moral justification but rather consisted of a belief that the moral quality of the law was irrelevant to its validity as law. Representatives of the German state practiced discrimination, the appropriation of property, and, eventually, the imprisonment and killing of innocent people as lawful activities.

At almost the same time, the law under Stalin's version of state socialism became a tool for a dictatorship framed as "the progressive dictatorship of the proletariat." The will of Stalin—presented as the embodiment of the interests of both the Communist Party and the working class—was regarded as a sufficient foundation for the law.

This historical background helps us to understand why many European theorists and practitioners of law are unwilling to reduce the controversy between natural law and legal positivism to an entirely conceptual enterprise. The issue at stake here is not only the concept of valid law. Theorizing the law also means offering instruments for a critique of the law in order to address the question: "Under what conditions are valid legal regulations morally justified?" Many legal positivists follow British philosopher H. L. A. Hart, who most clearly expressed the idea that legal positivism should contribute to a moral critique of law. Valid law can be profoundly immoral, and any theorist of law who recognizes this fact is required to offer a moral and political critique of the law.

In what follows, I will argue that legal positivism can and should be framed in such a way that the moral justification of legal regulations is preserved as an element of the theory of modern law. Obviously, what constitutes moral justification is a matter of reasonable disagreement—most importantly, between proponents of legal positivism and natural law theory. While natural law theorists defend the idea of natural morality as something that should guide the legislator, legal positivists are skeptical about its very existence.

How then should we make a moral critique of the law? In my view, a plausible approach to such a project should incorporate the insight that the relationship between the legal validity of norms and the moral quality of those norms cannot be understood without paying attention to politics as an arena for both legislation and critique of the law. Most legal positivists view politics and legislation through the lens of political realism, thereby distancing themselves from the political moralism of natural law. This political moralism contains the claims that moral considerations are fundamental to political action and that ethics as a theoretical reflection on morality should guide political agency and, most importantly legislative practice.[3] In contrast to this political moralism, most legal positivists view the law as a product of the exercise of power—that is, of politics driven by different interests rather than moral convictions.

Who is right and how do different positions on the nature of politics influence the discussion of law and morality? Let us start by admitting that skepticism of natural law and its political moralism does not necessarily mean embracing political cynicism. As Swedish ethicist Carl-Henric Grenholm has demonstrated, we should discriminate between political realism on the one hand and political cynicism on the other. Political realism accepts the idea that politics is a particular practice of gaining, sustaining, and increasing power, but it does not exclude morality as a relevant factor for political agents. According to political cynicism, politics and morality are wholly separated.

One prominent example of political cynicism that Grenholm examines is Carl Schmitt's view of politics and morality. According to Schmitt, politics and morality are two wholly separate arenas. Politics is defined by the distinction between friend and foe, which explains why morality has no relevance for political action. To consolidate a democracy according to Schmitt demands a majoritarian consensus on who constitutes the foe(s) of a particular state and a readiness to exclude or even eliminate them regardless of their actual deeds. Moral judgments are irrelevant for politics—they are extraneous to the very essence of politics ("the political" in Schmitt's terminology).

Political realists such as Hans J. Morgenthau and Reinhold Niebuhr endorse the idea that politics is defined by material interests and conflicts. To act politically is to act in order to gain, sustain, and increase power. At the same time, and in clear opposition to Schmitt, both Morgenthau and Niebuhr argue that morality does have relevance for political actions. Politics is not beyond morality, even if political morality differs from ordinary individual ethics.[4]

In what follows, I will utilize Grenholm's approach to political realism and political cynicism in order to discuss different versions of legal positivism. It is possible to make a cogent argument that there exists no natural morality that can serve as a basis for legal validity *and* that positive law, being a product of the exercise of power, should be subjected to moral scrutiny. To achieve this aim, we should look for an understanding of morality beyond both the trans-political metaphysics of natural law and the value nihilism that is incorporated into some forms of legal positivism.[5]

My investigation will be pursued in three steps. First, I will analyze three forms of legal positivism that, as I see it, offer resources for the moral and political critique of legal regulations. British philosopher Herbert L. A. Hart (1907–1992), British-Israeli philosopher Joseph Raz (1939–2022), and German philosopher Jürgen Habermas (born 1929) develop approaches to law that combine a theory of legal validity with ethical theory and political theory. Thus, my first step will be to interpret the dialectics of law, morality, and politics in Hart, Raz, and Habermas. In order to fulfill this first task, I will interpret and clarify their various understandings of positive law, conventional morality, critical morality, and democratic politics.

Second, I will engage in a critical dialogue with these three authors and argue that if legal positivism is to operate as an effective critical position, it needs to incorporate a more plausible understanding of morality—conventional as well as critical. I will interpret—sometimes even reconstruct—these theorists' positions on normative ethics and ethical theory;[6] and I will suggest an alternative position. Third, I will discuss different views of democratic politics that, when combined with legal positivism, either weaken or strengthen its critical potential.

## LEGAL POSITIVISM AS A CRITICAL THEORY

Accordingly, in this study, it is assumed that to understand the law is to understand the dialectics of law, morality, and politics. If compared to current trends in legal philosophy, my project can be seen as an attempt to reclaim the classical model of legal philosophy, which explicitly related the analysis of the law to the analysis of morality and politics.

Of course, legal positivists embrace particular and different views of morality and politics. However, many philosophers of law regard this embracement as contingent upon or even irrelevant to the design of legal positivism as a theory of law. It is presupposed then, that such a theory must constitute a theorization of positive law. Let us take an example.

In the introduction to a companion to legal positivism co-edited by Swedish philosophers Patricia Mindus and Torben Spaak, descriptive legal positivism is regarded as the central form of legal positivism. This descriptive positivism is, the editors claim, "an analytical theory that concerns the concept of law, or the nature of law, or both."[7] Introducing an impressive collection of essays on various forms of legal positivism, its central figures, tenets, and critics, the editors contend that legal positivism is a position on positive law (or on a theory of positive law) rather than a theory of the relationship between law, morality, and politics. Thus, the positivity of law is not only a defining feature of modern law but is also viewed as *the* legitimate object of legal theory.

Clearly inspired by Joseph Raz's understanding of central controversies in legal positivism,[8] Mindus and Spaak offer the following description of legal positivism:

> Even though legal positivists differ on a number of issues, most of them accept three central tenets, namely, the social thesis, the separation thesis and the thesis of social efficacy. In addition, some legal positivists accept a fourth thesis, called the semantic thesis. Crudely put, the social thesis has it that what is law and what is not is a matter of social fact; the separation thesis says that there is no necessary connection between law and morality; the thesis of social efficacy says that the validity (or existence) of law presupposes that the law is socially efficacious; and the semantic thesis has it, in one version, that legal normative or evaluative terms such as "right," "duty" and "authority" have different meanings (senses) from the corresponding moral terms and, in another version, that (first-order) legal statements are statements solely about social facts.[9]

Although legal positivism, as understood in the companion, can be combined with different positions within moral philosophy and political theory, such combinations do not impact the substance of legal positivism as an analytical theory of law.

In practice, however, many contributors to the companion, including Spaak himself, recognize the importance of the moral-philosophical elements of legal positivism, especially those of a metaethical character. Among the most obvious ethical elements of legal positivism is a rejection of moral realism and cognitivism. The endorsement of "true morality" cannot be combined with any version of legal positivism, the editors claim.[10] The social thesis and the separation thesis are not compatible with moral realism and cognitivism. We can agree on that.

However, the rejection of moral realism and cognitivism should not be taken to mean that the factual moral conventions of a society are the only kind of morality to which legal positivists should pay attention in their theories of law. Alternative metaethical positions on critical morality exist, and these positions have significant implications for legal positivism as a theory of modern law. Later, I will defend a non-cognitivist understanding of critical morality. For now, it is important to realize that whenever legal positivists take a stand on the issue of morality, critical morality, or politics—and they often do, either explicitly or implicitly—they are in practice interpreting law as a phenomenon that is dialectically related to both morality and politics.

The authors of the companion, all well-established specialists on legal positivism, have made a significant effort to bring greater conceptual clarity to the scholarly discussion of legal positivism. Such clarity greatly enhances the analytical approach to the theory of law. However, it also risks delimiting our analysis in such a way that the critical dimension of law—its relation to politics and morality—remains undertheorized.

Contrary to the paradigm presented in the volume edited by Spaak and Mindus, which excludes explicit theorizing of morality and politics from the scope of legal positivism, I will argue that legal positivism as a theory of modern law changes sufficiently when combined with different understandings of morality and politics. This is so because legal positivism is a tradition that aspires to offer an alternative to natural law—to explain the relationship between law, morality, and politics.[11]

In practice, most legal positivists develop views of morality and politics that exceed the framework as described in terms of the four tenets in the preceding quotation from Mindus and Spaak. Even more importantly, if legal positivism is a theory of law, and thus a theory of how law is related to and distinct from politics and morality, this theory should not be based on contingent views on politics and morality.

Finally, a plausible theory of modern law should not be wholly descriptive. Law is a social institution and a plausible theory of law must offer instruments for scrutinizing this institution.

Let us consider the case of Herbert L. A. Hart, whose coherent and elegant version of legal positivism combines the separation thesis with the idea that law should be subjected to moral critique. As I will demonstrate in the chapter on Hart, his theory of law is based on an explicitly articulated belief that the moral critique of positive law is a crucial practice for democracy. Most important is Hart's view that the very positivity of law, for instance, the distinction between legal validity and moral legitimacy, counteracts social conformism and encourages a democratic critique of law. Awareness of the existence of unjust but legally valid regulations is a democratic resource for the progressive reform of legislation.

When Hart was developing and defending his version of legal positivism, his utilitarianism and liberalism became important components of the theory. Moreover, as will be demonstrated in my analysis of Hart, his legal positivism incorporates metaethical assumptions that to a large degree define the critical potential of his theory. According to Hart, the moral critique of law is a key part of democratic politics, for which reason he is skeptical of any theory that incorporates the criterion of moral legitimacy into its test of legal validity. In so doing, natural law risks misleading citizens into viewing all valid legal norms as morally justified.

Citizens of society as Hart envisions it—a community of individuals as well as politically organized agents—should be aware of the separation thesis and recognize legal regulations as binding without treating legal demands as identical to moral obligations. For Hart, moral legitimacy is always a matter of moral justification and therefore a resource for the development of positive law.

In my reading of Hart, as in my reading of Joseph Raz and Jürgen Habermas, their particular understandings of the separation thesis presuppose *particular* views of morality and politics. In what follows, I will interpret these views and demonstrate how they contribute to the critical potential of legal positivism as a theory of modern law.

Thus, my main purpose is to argue in favor of legal positivism as a theory of law, morality, and politics. Such a theory offers a dialectical account of modern law and is therefore more plausible than a purely descriptive theory. This theory is also a powerful tool for the critique of law. I disagree with scholars such as David Dyzenhaus, who believes that the separation thesis distorts the project of philosophy of law that "understand[s] how a legal order can vindicate its claim to be an order of legitimate authority."[12] Instead, I will show how the separation thesis can serve such a purpose.

There are of course scholars whose approaches to law are similar to mine. Among the theorists discussed in this book, Habermas offers the most elaborated argument in favor of a dialectical and critical theory of modern law. Of particular importance for my analysis is the fact that Habermas does not reduce the law, or the scrutiny of law, to a practice of adjudication. Instead, he analyzes the law from the perspective of democratic citizens. The practice of legislation is therefore crucial in Habermas's approach to normative quality of modern law. In what follows, I will interpret Habermas's critical theory of modern law as it relates to morality and politics while also suggesting some revisions to it.

Finnish legal theorist Kaarlo Tuori has conducted a similar project by adapting Habermas's discourse theory to reclaim legal positivism as a critical theory of modern law. In his monograph *Critical Legal Positivism*, Tuori focuses on the positivity of modern law as a defining feature and a challenge of modernity. In its fundamental positivity, modern law differs from natural law theories on the one hand and from traditionalistic legal cultures on the other. Variations of natural law contain non-posited criteria of the legitimacy of social regulations. Natural morality is presupposed to legitimate legal regulations as well as limit them. Variations of traditional law legitimize and limit legal rulers by means of particular traditions that codify proper human conduct. How then should we draw the boundaries of legitimacy for wholly positive law? How is a normative critique of law possible when neither natural nor traditional morality is viewed as its moral foundation? These are the questions that critical positivism must address. As Tuori writes:

> I call my conception of modern law and legal science *critical legal positivism*. My objective is to formulate and justify an alternative to the traditional legal positivism [. . .] Traditional legal positivism is not able to answer certain fundamental questions about the law which gain in importance under the conditions of modern law, culture, and society. These are questions of the *limits* and the *criteria of the legitimacy* of the law.[13]

Thus, Tuori's alternative version of legal positivism emphasizes the fundamental positivity of modern law, which implies a firm rejection of both traditionalistic justifications of law and the natural law model. However, it differs from many forms of legal positivism in that critical legal positivism recognizes the crucial importance of a normative critique of legal regulations. Critical legal positivism, Turoi explains, "relativises the separation of 'Is' and 'Ought' [within legal practice]. [C]ritical positivism also rejects the strict separation between law and morals."[14]

How exactly is Tuori's approach different from natural law? The answer is that critical legal positivism handles the issue of limits and legitimacy of positive law in such a way that the fundamental positivity of social norms (of modernity) is coherently preserved. Such preservation is possible when we admit that all kinds of social norms are conventional and still possible to critically approach. The demarcation between morality and law is not a demarcation between pre-given norms of "true" morality and posited norms of law. Law may differ from morality but it always contains normative principles of justification in its deep structure. It is here that Tuori draws on Habermasian discourse theory: "In critical legal positivism [it is impossible to step outside positive law because] the ultimate criteria of validity—the principles of justification sedimented into the law's deep structure—partake in the positivity of modern law."[15]

Thus, in Tuori's analysis, the law has a complex structure. To substantially justify the law, it is necessary to scrutinize it "in the light of the morally and ethically laden principles of the law's sub-surface layers."[16] Such justification connects legal practice in the strict sense with scrutiny of law on behalf of citizens.

Tuori recognizes the fact that modern law, if understood as a complex social phenomenon, cannot be reduced to a legal practice conducted by professionals trained in particular legal cultures. In a modern democracy, the perspective of citizens, both as authors of legitimate legal regulations and as objects of legal regulations that can be coercively imposed on them by the state, is crucial. Despite not being a critique from the perspective of the lawyer (as lawyer), a normative critique of law from the perspective of citizens is therefore not an external critique. Instead, it is an internal perspective that preserves the fundamental positivity of law while simultaneously subjecting it to a moral and political critique that does not require belief in a "true morality," whether traditionalistic or natural.

While I agree with Tuori on this issue, I use a different approach to critical legal positivism. My version of critical legal positivism emphasizes and develops dialectical resources in the late Habermas of *Between Facts and Norms* rather than his earlier theory of discourse and his understanding of speech acts. As a legal theorist, Tuori is mostly interested in the implications of his critical positivism for legal practice in *sensu stricto*. Relying on Habermas's discourse theory in matters of politics and morality, Tuori discusses the limits and criteria of the legitimacy of law from "his position of a participant in legal practices."[17] In my approach to the issue of legitimacy of law, citizens as authors of the law are equally important. Legal practice is a particular social practice with particular professional expertize connected to it, but it should be scrutinized from different perspectives.

My point of departure is ethics as a critical study of social morality. What are the limits and criteria of legitimacy of modern law as defined by its fundamental positivity? I will answer this question from the perspective of a critical ethicist who understands the modern law through the lens of a dialectics between the social phenomena of law, morality, and politics.

## CONVENTIONAL AND CRITICAL MORALITY

In this investigation, my most important task is to define the conditions under which modern law is morally justified. I pose this question as an ethicist who recognizes the fundamental positivity of the law and simultaneously endorses the importance of moral and political critique of law.

There are two particularly important dimensions of the "critical" in the context of my investigation. One has to do with my understanding of ethics as a philosophical critique of morality. Another is the assumption that unjust social conventions appear as such to those whose material positions expose injustice precisely as being injustice.

Ethics is a philosophical and therefore critical inquiry, and its object is morality. How ethicists understand the phenomenon of morality is crucial to the character of the critique they deliver. In my view, morality is a social phenomenon that comprises two levels, one conventional and the other critical. To begin with, morality is a dimension of social relations, an instrument that regulates individual and collective actions. Conventions about good and bad, and right and wrong, are powerful tools for socialization into communities as well as mechanisms of social exclusion. Typically, moral conventions preserve existing social systems; they regulate cooperation in terms of already established social structures. However, moral ideas can become instruments of social critique, reforms, and even revolutions.

Let us consider the already-mentioned example of contemporary Islamophobia in Europe. Anti-Muslim racism efficiently invokes presupposed moral values of European democracies in order to exclude or assimilate Muslim minorities. It is often claimed that the integration of Muslims into democratic societies of Europe demands those Muslims' conversion from "Islamic values" to democratic ones. The idea of democratic values as part of personal morality legitimizes the politics of assimilation, but it is also used in order to present migrants from Islamic cultures as a threat to institutions of European democracies (such as taxation, education, health care, etc.). This, in turn, is presented as the objective of restrictive migration laws. Serious violations of the humanitarian law and human rights are thereby legitimized by the claim that Islamic morality is incompatible with democratic institutions.

Critics of anti-Muslim racism adopt several strategies when responding. Descriptively, it is clear that the idea of "democratic morality" as individual value orientation is used by those who, although not always reflexively, equate democracy with an aggregation of preferences on behalf of European majorities. The assumption of shared moral values—usually the idea of individual freedom of choice as the fundamental value—becomes an instrument for the inclusion of some and exclusion of others. In this construction of democracy as a moral identity of majorities, human rights are efficiently transformed from a matter of legal regulations of the state's obligations toward individuals and minorities into a matter of personal morality.

On the normative level, however, many critics condemn Islamophobia as a form of racism, that is, a way of treating humans that is fundamentally immoral. Human rights are here understood as principles of political morality and used in order to expose unjust social institutions, including legal regulations.[18] Obviously, moral arguments are used by both sides in the debate.[19] This can be done pragmatically—in order to influence public opinion—or sincerely. It is of course possible to have both motives.

How then should we discuss morality in the context of contemporary political developments? Ethics as a critical analysis of morality stipulates that the moral dimension of democratic institutions is not a matter of individual morality. Discourses on individual morality are usually compatible with unjust social structures. Moreover, a focus on standards of individual morality in many cases legitimizes existing social structures and social injustice. Unjust warfare is often presented as justified by the patriotism of individuals, their personal courage, and self-sacrifice.

The real question for democratic deliberation and ethical inquiry is therefore "What kind of social-ethical criteria should be fulfilled in order for institutional solutions to be morally justified?"

To address this question, we must distinguish between merely conventional and critical morality. Conventional morality refers to norms, principles, and values that regulate human actions in different societies and that can be described from the perspective of an observer. Some of these conventions are included in the legislation, others function in a much less formalized manner. In any case, conventional morality is always a product of concrete forms of social cooperation. In my analysis of legal positivism, I endorse a form of social constructivism as an explanation of conventional morality. This constructivism states that moral norms, principles, and values exist as a dimension of social relations. Like those scholars of law who believe that a critique of law should take the form of a critique of the modes of social cooperation served by the law,[20] I believe that moral conventions are fundamentally an instrument of the concrete forms of social relations, cooperative as well as conflictual.

Moral norms, principles, and values exist as dimensions of social reality, which means that they are not constructed by individuals. Even on a collective level, moral conventions tend to be difficult to change, and certainly more difficult than legal conventions. On the other hand, the plurality of social positions and perspectives "within" a social reality explains how different moral conventions as well as critical approaches to such conventions emerge and become political factors. As we have seen in the example of contemporary Islamophobia in Europe, conventional understandings of human rights as fundamentally related to post-Christian European culture are being challenged by those who either become an object of racism or who regard racism toward the other as unjust. This challenge, which, in many cases, is presented as a struggle for justice, is obviously a social and political factor involving both cooperation and conflict.

A preliminary comparison of moral conventions and positive law reveals a significant ambivalence within conventional morality. On the one hand, and almost uncontestedly, moral conventions cannot be changed in the same way as positive law can be introduced and changed: moral conventions are more stable and often resist political and legal attempts to change them. While legal changes are regulated by the explicit procedural rules of particular societies (with the exception of revolutionary situations), changes to moral conventions are the result of a far more complex social dynamics. On the other hand, moral conventions, at least conventions in modern societies, do not aspire to the same kind of authority that is a condition of positive legislation. What is stipulated by valid law is intended to be enacted regardless of the grievances that people and groups may have against particular legal regulations. Morality, by contrast, is open ended and both can be and is contested. This is so because moral norms, values, and ideals are objects of practical discourse in which reasoning is (or expected to be) at least as relevant as authority based on tradition or power. To the extent that demands for the justification of conventional morality are recognized as legitimate, critical morality acquires political energy.

This ambivalence of morality, both as an instrument of the preservation of the status quo and as a resource for social change, is important when we analyze the relationship between morality, politics, and law. Of particular interest for this study are the moral conventions that become part of positive legislation and are therefore regarded both as binding in an authoritative sense and as subject to scrutiny by practical reason.

One example of such legislation is the legal prohibition of discrimination. International human rights law includes this prohibition as the guiding principle for the interpretation and implementation of all human rights. Naturally, countries use different strategies to incorporate the prohibition into their legal systems. It would seem, however, that numerous agents contest the understanding of which particular kinds of discrimination should be legally prohibited. Different minorities defend the view that minority status demands firm protection against discrimination, while critics of patriarchal structures wish to radicalize the legal regulation of gender equality.

Different perspectives on social morality significantly impact the way in which legal protections against discrimination are assessed. The European Network of Equality Bodies (*Equinet*) has published important studies of strategic litigation, for instance, the identification and pursuit of legal cases as part of a strategy to defend human rights, in discrimination law cases that demonstrate how political, moral, and legal perspectives on discrimination are interrelated. Strategic litigation is itself an attempt to incorporate relevant moral political perspectives, such as experiences of racism as a violation of human dignity, into the legal cultures of European countries.[21]

In order to scrutinize different approaches to the relationship between politics, morality, and law, I will therefore pay special attention to how theorists understand moral conventions. What kind of conventions are discussed and what kind of conventions are left behind? Are both individual and collective dimensions of conventional morality included in a particular analysis? Is morality understood rationalistically, as mostly a matter of cognitive activity, or as a dimension of social practice? Theories discussed in this study have different perspectives on conventional morality and, naturally, those perspectives are only partly explicated in the material. This gives an ethicist like myself an opportunity to critically approach models of legal positivism. Does Hart's theory of law and its relation to politics and morality survive the test of expanding its scope beyond the moral conventions that regulate the personal life of individuals? How, if at all, can it be modified in order to avoid reducing morality to private morality? Why is the category of social justice absent in Raz's theory, which initially aspires to justify a critique of law in terms of a critique of particular forms of social cooperation?

Those who endorse social constructivism in relation to conventional morality differ in their views on whether there is such a thing as critical morality. Contemporary forms of natural law theory are often an effort to combine the recognition of different moral contexts with the belief in natural morality as *the* critical level of morality. Morality is understood as embedded in concrete and different contexts. Simultaneously, the presupposed existence of universal human nature allows human reason to transcend context-dependency and to some extent grasp moral law beyond the power of particular conventions. For many ethicists within natural law tradition, the universality of reason consists in its capacity to discriminate between such contextual practices that dignify humanity and practices that obviously violate human dignity. The primary function of natural law is thus to scrutinize conventional norms—subject them to review by practical reason.

The rationalism of the natural law tradition, though modified,[22] remains an element of Kantianism even in its contemporary modes, such as the work of Rawls or Habermas. Human reason—either monological or communicative—is capable of discriminating between conventional norms that can withstand scrutiny by tests of universalizability[23] and those that fail such a test. As already mentioned, the belief in the existence of natural morality that universal reason can grasp significantly impacts how we understand the relationship between morality, politics, and law. Although positive law is closely linked to conventional norms, it is a natural universal morality that is used in order to scrutinize the normative quality of the law.

Social constructivism as framed within Marxism, feminism, and critical theory does not accept the existence of natural morality. Where, then, should a constructivist locate critical morality? The starting point of this investigation is a belief that we should look for critiques of conventional morality in social perspectives and positions that are immanent to contextual social practices. The main idea is that social reality, though defined by material factors such as economic and power relations, appears differently from different practical perspectives. Racism that is normalized and thus invisible to many is revealed as a form of injustice and a violation of human dignity when the experiences of its objects are articulated. Patriarchy appears as a system of domination from the perspective of those who are subjected to its domination.

A critical perspective on conventional norms is therefore practical and related to the experiences of the unprivileged in every particular social setting. In order to become an element of critical morality, insights on behalf of the unprivileged must be expressed and communicated in the society. In art, science, and, most importantly, in public democratic space, marginalized perspectives can gain the power to question established conventional morality—to demand justification for conventional morality as incorporated into positive law but also outside it.

One example of a political critique of law grounded in this understanding of morality is Hermann Heller's debate with Carl Schmitt. Heller, a philosopher of law and a social democrat, was troubled by the development in Germany that he described as "authoritarian liberalism." In Heller's analysis, Carl Schmitt's position on the constitutional crisis in Germany legitimized the alliance between ideologists of economic liberalism who wanted to save private capital from the power of the state and defenders of authoritarianism who strove to secure the state's control over society.[24]

Heller famously rejected Carl Schmitt's conceptualization of democratic politics "that declares rules and norms as insignificant" and "seeks to present the state of exception as the true and proper ordinary state, and to espouse the permanent autocratic dictatorship, unrestricted to emergencies, as the true democracy."[25] On the one hand, Heller analyzed social and economic developments in Germany in realistic terms, focusing on the material interests behind the political agents of the constitutional crises, including conservatives, economic liberals, and social democrats. On the other hand, he argued that a moral critique of law could be grounded in the contextual resources of the political community. Heller's critique of the pragmatic support for Hitler by conservative politicians did not presuppose the existence of natural morality. In the words of David Dyzenhaus,

> [Heller] does not equate the legitimacy of law with the instantiation of any particular set of moral values, although his thesis about the legitimacy of law does rest on a connection between law and morality. The moral value which he says law serves is the value of collective self-government—of citizens deciding together on the terms of their common life, subject always to proviso that the terms will require revisions in the light of experience.[26]

As a socialist, Heller believed that social equality constitutes citizenship, which, in turn, is fundamental for a functioning democracy. However, as a democrat, he believed that his defense of a socialist model of democracy, as with the defense of any other ideological model, had to be mounted by means of open political deliberation.[27] In sharp contrast to the political liberalism of John Rawls, Heller believed that there is no such a thing as moral principles that offer a trans-ideological framing for constitutional essentials in a democracy. Liberal rights and freedoms can be considered as constitutional essentials, but only as one position on political morality among others.

We will return to the issue of political liberalism as a background to some forms of legal positivism. For now, I want to highlight that in order to scrutinize different models of legal positivism I will pose a set of questions that explicate theorists' understanding of resources for the moral critique of law. Are these resources to be found in particular social practices and special sorts of social agency? If so, which practices and what kinds of agency?

As already stated, my ambition is to propose an understanding of political morality and ethics that strengthens the critical potential of legal positivism as a theory of modern law in relation to morality and politics. In order to succeed in this task, I will develop further a social constructivist view of critical morality. Such a view need not be identical with a value nihilism that rejects the possibility (or meaning) of rational evaluation of moral judgment. In my view, value nihilism is an erroneous position because it assumes that justification presupposes moral judgments to be either true or false. While my version of constructivism is similar to value nihilism in its rejection of objective values, I believe that moral judgments can be reasonable, even if they are not true.

I will therefore argue that it is possible to combine ethical constructivism with a metaethical position that can account for a reasonable, albeit never "pure" rational, justification of moral rules, values, and norms. Additionally, I will discuss normative ethics incorporated into different theories of modern law: utilitarianism in Hart; Aristotelianism in Raz; and discourse ethics in Habermas.

## THREE THEORIES OF LAW AND MORALITY

To realize the main goal of this book, I will engage in a discussion with Hart, Raz, and Habermas. I will interpret and scrutinize their respective understandings of the relation between law, morality, and politics. Furthermore, I will explicate their views on conventional and critical morality. Finally, I will discuss their approach to democratic politics as the domain where morality and law interact.

Let me explain my choice of theorists. To begin with, there are significant similarities between Hart, Raz, and Habermas as regards how they approach modern law in its relation to politics and morality. These similarities allow me to focus my analysis theoretically as well as contextually.

Both Hart and Raz understand the relationship between law, morality, and politics within the paradigm of legal positivism as I use the term in this investigation. They separate the issue of the legal validity of positive regulations from the question of the moral quality of law even while at the same time endorsing the social and legal importance of the moral scrutiny of law. Habermas believes that his theory of law, in combination with a particular form of discourse ethics, transcends the dichotomy between natural law and legal positivism. In my reading, however, Habermas's theory of modern law, including, most importantly, his firm critique of the "Platonism of natural law," is a form of legal positivism.[28]

All three theorists are explicitly interested in the role of law and political morality in contemporary Western democracies. The law is understood by Hart, Raz, and Habermas as fundamental to a democratic order that they envision as liberal democracy in the European or North American mode. All three work trans-disciplinarily, for instance, combining their respective analysis of law with philosophical and sociological analyses of politics and morality.

Additionally, Hart, Raz, and Habermas all offer explicit discussions of the controversy between natural law and legal positivism beyond a purely conceptual investigation of positive law, legal validity, and moral justification. In their writings, the social complexity of modern societies and legal systems is not sacrificed for the sake of analytical purity. In my view, this priority has to do with the fact that all three theorists aspire to contribute to the institutional analysis of social cooperation and conflict.

Alongside these and other similarities, there exist differences between Hart, Raz, and Habermas that, as I see it, define their particular framing of the relationship between law, politics, and morality. One of the most salient differences in this study is ideological in nature. Hart offers a transparent defense of classical liberalism and develops an understanding of the law that supports what he depicts as a progressive liberal democracy. Both the subject and the object of progressive democratic politics are, as Hart theorizes it, the private individual. As we will see in the chapter on Hart, he makes a considerable effort to justify the need for private morality, not least sexual morality, to remain free from legal constraints and the administrative involvement of the state.

Like Hart, Raz views individuals as counterparts to the state with regard to issues of democratic politics, morality, and law. In contrast to Hart, however, Raz incorporates a communitarian perspective in his analysis of personal freedom in relation to the power of the state. For Raz, existential and moral choices can be considered free only when people are given access to particular contexts of meaningful opportunities. In his opinion, the state has an obligation to secure a reasonable measure of meaningful choice opportunities for the individual. In Raz's perfectionist liberalism, personal freedom and the relationship between the individual and state power are thus different in kind to those of Hart's version of liberalism.

According to both Hart and Raz, the state operates in relation to individuals who, in turn, seek to promote their personal goals and projects within the framework of the modern legal system and pluralistic morality. Habermas, on the other hand, understands freedom as social agency and therefore focuses his analysis of law and morality on collective practices rather than personal protection from the power of the state. Like Hart and Raz, Habermas uses the category of legally enacted rights in order to explain and scrutinize the relationship between the personal and the political. In contrast to Hart and Raz, Habermas envisions rights as a matter of democratic agency—the construction of citizenship as political subjectivity—rather than merely the state's obligations that correspond to individual liberties.

Another important difference between the three theorists has to do with the kind of law that each of them is mostly preoccupied with. On one hand, all three aspire to formulate a general theory of modern law.[29] On the other hand, they naturally focus on different types of law when discussing the issue of legal validity as well as the moral quality of the law. Hart has argued powerfully against the tendency of the older legal positivism to view criminal law as paradigmatic for any law and to thereby overestimate the importance of sanctions. In his *Concept of Law* Hart agrees with those who believe that properly functioning legal regulations must effectively be accepted by the general public and officials rather than rely on obedience in the face of a threat of sanctions.[30] This becomes obvious, Hart claims, if we extend our analysis of law beyond the context of criminal law. As Hart notes in relation to the issue of the variety of laws:

> The power thus conferred on individuals to mould their legal relations with others by contracts, wills, marriages, &c., is one of the great contributions of law to social life; and it is a feature of law obscured by representing all law as matter of orders backed by threats. The radical difference in function between law that confer such powers and the criminal stature is reflected in much of our normal ways of speaking about this class of laws.[31]

Raz endorses and further develops Hart's concept of law, focusing, among other things, on the dynamic of parochial and universal dimensions of the concept of law.[32] However, it is less obvious what kind of law Raz prioritizes in his general analysis. Habermas deals mostly with constitutional and public law.[33] He endorses Ronald Dworkin's interpretative theory of law, which states that adjudication in hard cases should be pursued in the light of constitutional principles that are political and moral in nature. Legal norms must be constructively interpreted by judges who strive for the preservation of the integrity of fundamental constitutional principles. Although Habermas is less sympathetic than Dworkin to judges' monopoly on the interpretation of constitutional principles, he views constitutional principles as a kind of justificatory dimension of law.[34] Like Hart and Raz, he comments on the relationship between national legal systems and international law (human rights law in the first place) without elaborating on the issue at length.

In short, I assume that careful analysis of the different understandings of the relationship between law, politics, and morality requires us to pay attention to which parts of legal systems are being examined or viewed as paradigmatic. This implies that we also make a note of possible blind spots in the theorists' models of law. As we will see, none of the main theorists in this study takes a critical approach to the issue of how economic relations are legally structured under different forms of advanced capitalism, a lacuna that invites us to consider the question of how to transform legal positivism in order to incorporate this crucial aspect of legal regulation into our analysis.[35]

## FROM LIBERALISM'S SOFT JUSTICE TO DEMOCRACY WITHIN CAPITALIST CONSTRAINTS

This investigation starts with a short discussion of the natural law tradition. We will focus on two versions of natural law theory. The first one is that of Jean Porter, an American theologian and ethicist. It is traditional in the sense it follows and further develops the scholastic approach to morality and law. However, Porter makes a significant effort to combine traditional natural law theory with the promotion of cultural pluralism. The second version is that of another American scholar, Lon Fuller, who defends a theory of "internal morality" of law. Finally, I will turn to Ronald Dworkin's version of the morality of law. Since Dworkin is recognizably the most influential contemporary critic of legal positivism, it is of great interest to recapitulate his position in order to compare it with traditional natural law theory.

I will argue that natural law tradition does not offer a plausible understanding of the dynamics of law, morality, and politics. My main objections are directed to the value ontology of natural law theory, its cognitivism, and, finally, the idea that the moral quality of law constitutes a necessary criterion of its validity. I will conclude the chapter with a discussion of one of the most influential critics of the natural law tradition, the Swedish legal positivist Axel Hägerström. I will focus on his revision of Marxism and demonstrate why Hägerström is wrong when he states that embracing materialism requires us to embrace value nihilism.

My next step is to approach the theories of Hart, Raz, and Habermas as alternatives to natural law. What we are looking for is a theory that combines insights into the positivity of modern law with an acknowledgment of the moral critique of law. Such a critique does not presuppose the acceptance of value objectivism. Nor does it accept the cognitivism underpinning the natural law view of morality.

We will first turn to the classical form of soft legal positivism framed by Herbert L. A. Hart. As mentioned earlier, Hart argues that the very positivity of law, that is, the distinctiveness of legal validity in relation to moral legitimacy, counteracts social conformism and encourages the democratic critique of law.

Although Hart's legal positivism is compatible with political realism, it does not endorse cynicism in matters of political morality: he rejects the thesis that politics and morality are two strictly separated spheres of social life. Morality does play a role in Hart's understanding of politics. Additionally, contrarily to the value nihilists who argue that moral conventions are ultimately a matter of material interests and power, Hart believes that morality has two dimensions, one conventional and one critical. Conventional morality, not least when it assumes a legal form, confirms existing social relations, within which relations between the state and individuals are crucial for Hart's liberalism. The critical dimension of morality is different and should be utilized politically in order to change the law. For obvious reasons, Hart's utilitarian model of critical morality as a resource for scrutiny of law is of special importance for this study.

Hart's soft legal positivism, a novelty in his own historical context, was designed to be compatible with the view that the classical liberal understanding of freedom should guide the utilitarian enterprise of devising moral justifications for legal norms. While previous forms of legal positivism sustained the separation thesis on both descriptive and normative levels, Hart believes that the separation thesis allows and even promotes moral scrutiny of the coercion exercised by the state through its legal system. In my reading of Hart, precisely the coercion that states exercise toward individuals must be the object of justification even when the legality of the norms is confirmed.

In this study, the advantages as well as the weaknesses of this kind of liberal moral critique of law will be analyzed. I will argue that Hart makes a problematic reduction of critical morality—both when he focuses on freedom as the individual's freedom from coercion by the state and when he dismisses a theory of rights while endorsing utilitarianism as the most progressive form of normative ethics.

Joseph Raz defends and develops legal positivism at a time when political moralism—most prominently, the work of John Rawls—rather than political realism is widely regarded as the most persuasive position on politics and morality. By this point we have learned that, contrary to political realism, which recognizes morality as a dimension of politics while sharp differentiating between personal morality and the morality of collective agency, political moralism—at least of the type defended by Rawls—proposes one and the same set of criteria for morally justified political action. Furthermore, political moralism argues that normative ethics can guide political agency directly and, in this regard, differs from the understanding of the role of ethics as framed within critical theory.[36]

Raz supports political moralism by stating that the law always aspires to be a legitimate authority and that precisely this social fact makes a moral critique of law possible. Legal validity does not presuppose that legal norms are morally justified. However, the law as an authoritative reason for human actions, for instance, as binding even when wrong, necessarily *claims* its authority to be justified. This particular claim on behalf of authority creates a space for practical reason. Although it is in many cases reasonable to believe that the authoritative reasons given through law are justified, such reasons are not morally binding unless justified by practical reason. Thus, there is a fundamental difference in Raz between the nature of legal authority on one hand and moral legitimacy on the other.

I will discuss this approach and argue that it offers several advantages when compared with other forms of legal positivism. Additionally, Raz's theory of legal authority is combined with a clearly articulated approach to the relationship between law and other forms of social cooperation. Raz argues, rightly so in my view, that a critique of law should be a critique of concrete forms of social cooperation that the law seeks to promote.

In Raz's version of legal positivism, Hart's liberalism is substantially modified. Freedom on behalf of individuals presupposes that there exist reasonable alternatives for meaningful personal projects and choices. Such alternatives cannot be created by individuals themselves and must therefore be secured by the state and its law. In practice, this means that the state must preserve a variety of communities and traditions that allow for personal development. In what follows I offer an analysis of this modified version of liberalism. Does it offer efficient tools for a critique of law? I will argue that Raz's attempt to modify liberal ethics by incorporating elements from Aristotelian ethics does indeed challenge Hart's individualism. However, I will demonstrate that Raz's own theory poses a serious problem for readers looking for critical resources. This has to do with the fact that even fundamentally unjust and undemocratic social orders can offer meaningful alternatives for personal projects and, according to Raz, are therefore justified. Trying to incorporate communitarian insights into legal positivism, Raz in practice loses its most important normative element—the defense of democracy as politics of social transformations—or so I will argue.

Jürgen Habermas does not describe his theory of law as a form of legal positivism. In his efforts to explain the relationship between law, politics, and morality, he mostly focuses on modern democracy and aspires to overcome the controversy between natural law and legal positivism by means of a discourse theory of law and democracy. Habermas sees the dynamics of private and public autonomy[37] as the main advantage of a democracy that incorporates a system of rights into its constitution. In my reading, Habermas's constructivist approach to fundamental rights makes his position similar to Hart's legal positivism. This is despite the fact that, as I will later demonstrate, Habermas dogmatically endorses Dworkin's misrepresentation of Hart.

The main advantage of Habermas's approach in comparison with both Hart and Raz is the close attention that Habermas pays to how the public sphere is structured in contemporary democracy, which is, in turn, framed and limited by global financial capitalism. While Hart and Raz mostly focus on the state and individuals, Habermas regards the law as relevant to democratic structures that cannot be reduced to agencies of the state and individuals. When discussing the dynamic of legality and legitimacy Habermas offers an explicit account of modern democracy, including both its formal structure for decision-making and its formation of opinion in civil society as well as the public at large.

Along with an interpretative approach to Habermas's view of positive law in modern democracy, I offer a critique of his position. I do not believe that he overcomes the tension between natural law and positivism. Nor should he. This "tension" helps to sustain a dialectical approach to law, morality, and politics. In my reading of Habermas, precisely this dialectical approach is a major strength of his understanding of positive law and democratic politics.

Most importantly, I will discuss Habermas's approach to critical morality. Habermas rightly questions the belief that the critique of social conventions should be a philosophical enterprise. Political deliberation between real social agents in different democratic settings is the proper arena for such a critique, he claims. However, I will argue that, although philosophers should not aspire to the role of an expert in issues of political morality, they should not delimit their philosophical projects to the issue of formal justification structures. Ethical constructivism can and should be framed in ways that allow a philosophical critique of moral conventions both within and without the legal domain. It is true that social emancipation is always and necessarily political and contextual. But it is also true that moral philosophy can contribute to emancipatory practices.

Related to the discussion of the relationship between philosophical critiques of positive law and social conventions is the issue of Habermas's view of radical democracy. I will argue that it is not radical enough. Habermas underestimates the importance of legal regulations of the economic relations in contemporary capitalism and therefore, I argue, wrongly dismisses the category of social revolution[38] as irrelevant to the critical analysis of modern democracy, its politics, morality, and law. In my version of legal positivism, the possibility of radical changes in social and economic structures is crucial.

## CRITIQUE OF LAW: THEORY AND PRACTICE

The aim of this book is thus to defend a theory of law that recognizes the positivity of modern law as its fundamental feature while simultaneously offering the tools for a moral critique of law. My primary concern is not conceptual. Rather, I am concerned with how the dialectics of politics, law, and morality should be understood by scholars interested in a normative critique of legal regulations.

I will argue that legal positivism as a theory of modern law in its relation to politics and morality should be combined with a plausible understanding of conventional and critical morality. After presenting an analysis of three models of legal positivism, I will suggest a form of legal positivism that includes a constructivist account of both conventional and critical morality. Such a theory recognizes the positivity of modern law as its defining feature. Simultaneously it is critical. An account of modern law developed in this book provides some tools for exposing injustice.

The following chapter deals with the natural law tradition. It contains a short discussion of contemporary natural law theory that challenges legal positivism in several important regards. The very distinction between positive law and morally justified law is a legacy of natural law theories. Moreover, in a clear contrast to traditionalistic accounts of law, natural law theory offers resources for making a trans-contextual and rational scrutiny of legal regulations. However, natural law theory implies a view of natural morality that downplays the complexity of social morality. While this is true for the explicit versions of natural law found in the work of Jean Porter and John Finnis, it also holds for other critics of legal positivism such as Ronald Dworkin.

The three chapters following this section on natural law address the relationship between positive law, politics, and morality in Hart, Raz, and Habermas, respectively. Since it is beyond the scope of this study to give a complete picture of their work, my aim is rather to clarify the dialectics of law, politics, and morality by focusing on how each of these theorists understands conventional and critical morality. What resources are available for a critique of law in different models of legal positivism? How is morality understood and related to democratic and legal practices? Which interpretation of morality is most reasonable if legal positivism aspires to offer a critical perspective on the social realities of contemporary society?

Hopefully, my interpretations of Hart, Raz, and Habermas are generous and constructive. I proceed from the perspective of an ethicist, which allows me to pose questions to theorists of law that make explicit their unstated assumptions in the field of social morality and metaethics. As noted earlier, I believe that a theory of law that does not limit itself to mere descriptions of positive legislation and judicial practice must necessarily incorporate elements of moral philosophy and political theory. By focusing on these elements, I offer a more accurate understanding of the three theories of modern law.

In the last chapter of the book, I focus on the relationship between the critique of law as theoretical enterprise and critique as a social practice. We will return to Hart's initially crucial claim that precisely the positivity of law, its separation from morality, makes progressive critique of law possible. "Progressive" is naturally a relative depiction. At this point, let us stipulate that progressive critique is a critique of particular forms of social injustices that hide themselves under the veil of either natural order or social traditions. This critique aspires to transform the social institutions of a society in such a way that groups and individuals previously exposed to injustice can experience social cooperation as fair. Hart's liberal utilitarianism, for example, exposed the injustice of legal regulations of the private sphere in the United Kingdom. The fact that these regulations had been particularly harmful to sexual minorities made Hart's demands for reform progressive.

Hart finds resources for a progressive critique of law in classical utilitarianism, which, in contrast to the speculative approach of the natural law tradition, regards the interests of individuals as relevant for the critique of conventional norms and rules. Raz develops a modified Aristotelean model of social morality that seeks to overcome the individualistic reductionism of Hart's utilitarianism. Habermas takes the Hartian approach to modern law in yet another direction. In his search for resources for a critique of social conventions, he focuses on democratic collective agency in several different forms. This particular focus is crucial to discourse ethics as developed by Habermas in contradistinction to both Aristotelian and utilitarian ethics.

How critical is legal positivism's critique of law, then? I will argue that the critical potential of legal positivism can and should be radicalized. One way of doing that is to reframe legal positivism by means of a social constructivist account of morality. The social constructivism that will be defended in this book views moral conventions as secondary to material positions: unjust structures and relationships do not appear as unjust from any social position.

Because it is entirely natural to find it difficult to question the status quo when it supports one's own privileges, the experiences of the unprivileged are crucial to progressive social ethics. Economic injustice, social inequality, and contemporary racism are, as I see it, issues that must be addressed by this ethics.

Materialistically interpreted social constructivism should not, I argue, be equated with endorsement of value nihilism. Social injustices are only ever experienced in concrete material settings and perspectives. At the same time, any democratically powerful critique of injustice must include emancipatory visions that aspire for universal validity. I will be defending a particular model of moral universalism by arguing that such an account allows for a critique of positive law that is sensitive to the most urgent forms of social injustice.

The critique of Hart's, Raz's, and Habermas's respective understandings of the dialectics of law, politics, and morality in the last chapter of the book highlights their endorsement of democratic politics as an essentially reformative practice. Such a view of democracy excludes the possibility of radical change as a result of collective political agency. In contrast to this position, I will argue that legal positivism as a critical project should be combined with an understanding of politics that reclaims the category of social revolution, thereby endorsing constitutional agency on behalf of the unprivileged.

## NOTES

1. Kaarlo Tuori depicts the idea of positivity of modern law as follows: "Under the conditions of modern law, the law is conceived of as resulting from conscious human action." Kaarlo Tuori, *Critical Legal Positivism* (Milton Park, UK: Taylor and Francis, 2002), 6.

2. H. L. A. Hart, *The Concept of Law*. Third edition (Oxford, UK: Oxford University Press, 2012), 187.

3. Carl-Henric Grenholm, *Kritisk politisk etik. Om moralens betydelse inom politiken* (Uppsala: Acta Universitatis Upsaliensis, 2024), 19.

4. Ibid., 33–35.

5. One of the most prominent examples of such nihilism is an element of Axel Hägerström's (1868–1939) legal positivism. In Hägerström, legal positivism is combined with emotivism that rejects the existence of objective moral values. Further, moral judgments are understood as emotive expressions that can be neither true nor false. Moral judgments are defined by emotions that in turn are reflections of class-related material interests. See Axel Hägerström, *Socialfilosofiska uppsatser* (Stockholm: Bonniers, 1966), 109. In the next chapter, I will argue that although Hägerström's critique of the idea of objective values is reasonable, his emotivism wrongly dismisses the possibility of rational scrutiny of moral judgments. In what

follows, I will suggest a different form of non-cognitivism that combines ethical constructivism with a theory of rational justification of normative ethical positions.

6. I will use the terms metaethics and ethical theory interchangeably in this investigation. Although I prefer "ethical theory" for a theory of the semantics and justification of moral judgments, "metaethics" is a more frequent term in the literature.

7. Torben Spaak and Patricia Mindus, "Introduction," in *Cambridge Companion to Legal Positivism*, eds. Torben Spaak and Patricia Mindus (Cambridge, UK: Cambridge University Press, 2021), 12.

8. Joseph Raz, *The Authority of Law.* Second edition (Oxford, UK: Oxford University Press, 2009), 37–38.

9. Spaak and Mindus, "Introduction," 7.

10. Ibid., 9.

11. There are scholars who believe that legal positivism as the negation of natural law is mostly of historical importance. For example, Frederick Schauer argues that "of much greater importance is legal positivism as the negation of normatively undifferentiated decision-making." See Frederick Schauer, "Legal Positivism and the Contingent Autonomy of Law," in *Judicial Power, Democracy and Legal Positivism*, eds. Tom Campbell and and Jeffrey Goldsworthy (New York: Routledge, 2000), 216–217. I disagree with Schauer who reduces—mistakenly as I will demonstrate—legal positivism to a theory of adjudication. In this book, I follow theorists of law who construct legal positivism as a theory of law that includes adjudication as *one* dimension of modern law.

12. David Dyzenhaus, "Positivism and Totalitarianism," in *Cambridge Companion to Legal Positivism*, 783.

13. Tuori, *Critical Legal Positivism*, 8.

14. Ibid., 29.

15. Ibid., 263.

16. Ibid., 276.

17. Ibid., 4.

18. Madelene Persson, *Frågan om människovärde. En kritisk studie av mänskliga rättigheter i rasismens och migrationens tidevarv* (Uppsala: Acta Universitatis Upsaliensis, 2020).

19. For the sake of argument, I disregard the fact that there is a significant plurality of positions on the matter of democratic integration.

20. Joseph Raz, *Between Authority and Interpretation. On the Theory of Law and Practical Reason* (Oxford, UK: Oxford University Press, 2009), 101.

21. European Network of Equality Bodies, *Equinet Handbook on Strategic Litigation* (Equinet, 2017), 9.

22. While traditional reason discovers the natural law, modern Kantianism views reason as autonomous, i.e., self-legislative.

23. Later on in this study, we will discuss different understandings of universalizability test.

24. Hermann Heller, "Authoritarian Liberalism?" *European Law Journal* 21, no. 3 (2015): 295–301. German original 1933 *Die Neue Rundschau* 1933. See also Michael

Wilkinson, "Authoritarian Liberalism in the European Constitutional Imagination. Second Time as Farce?" *European Law Journal* 21, no 3. (2015): 313–339.

25. Ibid., 296.

26. David Dyzenhaus, *Legality and Legitimacy* (Oxford, UK: Oxford University Press, 1997), 204.

27. Ibid., 205–206.

28. Later on in this investigation, we will have a chance to compare Habermas's suggestion to dissolve the dichotomy of legal positivism and natural law with my strategy to broaden the scope of legal positivism as a theory of modern law.

29. In Hart's case even for a theory of any kind of law.

30. Hart, *The Concept of Law*, 116, 198.

31. Ibid., 28.

32. Raz, *Between Authority and Interpretation,* 31–36.

33. As we will see, Habermas discusses the relationship between public and private law. He does it in several contexts, such as, for example, the relationship between the state and the public sphere or the relationship between legal and substantial equality.

34. Jürgen Habermas, *Between Facts and Norms. Contributions to a Discourse Theory of Law and Democracy* (Cambridge, UK: Polity Press, 1996), 206–229.

35. There are several original studies on the issue of legal regulation of the contemporary form of capitalism. See Thomas Piketty, *Capital in the 21st Century* (Cambridge, MA: Harvard University Press, 2014); Katharina Pistor, *The Code of Capital. How the Law Creates Wealth and Inequality* (Princeton, NJ: Princeton University Press, 2019); Andreas Rahmatian, *Credit and Creed: A Critical Legal Theory of Money* (London: Routledge, 2019).

36. Grenholm, *Kritisk politisk etik*, 36–38.

37. *Between Facts and Norms* will be the main source for my interpretation of Habermas' position.

38. Jürgen Habermas, "Concluding remarks," in *Habermas and the Public Sphere*, ed. Craig Calhoun (Cambridge, MA: The MIT Press, 1992), 469.

# *Chapter 2*

# Beyond Natural Law

In this chapter, I will discuss some features of the contemporary natural law theory and explain why we should move beyond this theory when looking for resources for a moral critique of modern law.

As noted already, legal positivism is a theory of modern law that has emerged as an alternative to natural law. Many forms of legal positivism aspire to offer a better answer to the question of how positive law is related to morally justified law. In order to give such an answer, I argue, legal positivism as a theory of law should be combined with plausible normative ethics and ethical theory.

Obviously, a theorist of law can abstain from this task by focusing on a conceptual analysis of positive law and/or a descriptive perspective of law and legal practice. Hans Kelsen, for example, has argued that the theorist of law should not involve himself in the issue of moral justification.[1] Kelsen adopted this position because, in his view, a scientific moral justification of norms necessarily presupposes an embracing of cognitivism and positive value ontology. On this account, justifying norms means proving them true or false, which in turn implies the existence of objective values. In Kelsen's view, the theorist of law faces a dilemma: to acknowledge the relativity of moral conventions and therefore abstain from any discussion of justification, or to admit the existence of an absolute morality that alone allows for a scientifically reliable critique of law.[2]

This "absolute morality" is pre-given and universal in the sense that Christian natural law doctrine envisions morality. Kelsen claimed that the absolute morality of natural law cannot be applied to positive law by scholars of law, who should instead endorse moral relativism. As Kelsen writes: "the laws of natural law, derived [their validity] from nature, God or reason, from a principle of the absolutely good, right or just, from an absolutely supreme value or fundamental norm which itself is closed with the claim of absolute validity."[3]

Two objections must be raised against Kelsen in this particular regard. To begin with, Kelsen is wrong in claiming that moral justification is incompatible with an acknowledgment of descriptive moral relativism. It is true that moral norms are social conventions that differ between societies and groups. No absolute morality exists that can be used as a criterion for justification of moral conventions. However, this is not to say that a scientist who recognizes the truth of descriptive relativism cannot get involved in the issue of the moral justification of positive law. There are a variety of approaches to justification that neither presuppose the truth of traditional Christian value ontology nor include a cognitivism of the natural law tradition. In what follows, I discuss such approaches in Hart, Raz, and Habermas. In dialogue with them, I propose a modified version of social constructivism that endorses descriptive moral relativism while simultaneously allowing for a critical analysis of the moral conventions incorporated in legal regulations.

It should also be noted that the Christian value ontology that has been secularized in many Western philosophical accounts of law and morality is not the only version of religious morality that Kelsen dismisses altogether as in contradiction with the scientific understanding of morality. Both the Jewish and Muslim traditions offer a variety of views on the issue of divine law as it relates to human morality and politics. Although many Christian theologians and their secular heirs presuppose that universal moral law can only be given authoritatively, this is not how Judaism and Islam view the law.[4]

Furthermore, Kelsen's depiction of the positive value ontology and cognitivism as incorporated in the Christian tradition of natural law is overly polemical and unfair.[5] Natural law can be, and often is, combined with a reasonable account of descriptive moral pluralism. Moreover, contemporary natural law theorists seek to embrace moral pluralism as an ideal, thereby rising to the challenge of Jewish and Islamic theological approaches to moral pluralism. I will elaborate on these efforts in order to give a more accurate account of why theorists of law, though engaging in normative critique, should abandon natural law theory.

## NATURAL LAW AND THE CHALLENGE OF POSITIVE VALUE ONTOLOGY

Natural law theory can be framed in different ways but it always includes the claim that valid law must pass a test of rational moral justification. Some kind of pre-given natural morality—either metaphysical or rationalistic, or both—is the fundamental criterion for valid law. As Jean Porter puts it: "Formal law, understood along characteristically medieval and modern lines, is both justified and constrained by the *natural* purposes that it serves."[6]

Natural law theory, an element of Christian theology, includes a belief in the existence of a universal human nature that can be comprehended by reason. All human beings are created by God and all are images of that same God. In the context of natural law, therefore, everyone can attain moral knowledge. One does not need any particular revelation or access to a particular tradition: moral knowledge is knowledge of human nature as the reflection of God. Jean Porter describes the scholastic understanding of natural law:

> [. . . they developed] a view according to which the natural law is fundamentally a capacity or power to distinguish between good and evil; it is intrinsic to the character of the human soul as made in the Image of God, and therefore it cannot be altogether obliterated; and it is expressed or developed though moral precepts which are confirmed, as well as being completed and transcended, through the operation of grace.[7]

Thus, human reason, particularly the human capacity for moral judgment, is a reflection of God's wisdom. Scripture does not contradict reason but helps it to be "the supreme and definitive expression of divine wisdom."[8]

Contemporary natural law theory is often a rationalistic rather than metaphysical enterprise, and in many cases, it does not presuppose that the moral law grasped by human reason is static. A dynamic interpretation of the doctrine of natural law is the claim that universal moral law appears only through different contextual interpretations and applications. One example of such a reading of natural law is the hermeneutical realism of William Schweiker.[9] Although Schweiker does not reject the cognitivism incorporated into the natural law tradition, he reinterprets it through the lens of philosophical hermeneutics. Moral truths exist but never in pure universal forms: contextuality is always a dimension of true moral judgments.

Obviously, Christian ethics of natural law can be framed in more dynamic terms than its opponents typically depict it. There are also defenders of natural law that distance themselves from either Christian theology as a whole or significant parts of it. Before turning to them, let me explain why I still believe that theorists of law should reject classical natural law as an approach to the moral scrutiny of legal regulations.

Even when natural law theory is framed rationalistically and includes a dynamic view of both society and humanity, it still states that there is a universal human nature and a pre-given moral law that human reason can and should grasp. Let us consider Jean Porter's version of the classical natural law theory. In her view, human nature should be conceptualized "in terms of the intelligible principles structuring human activity seen on a descending scale of generality, from the level of our existence as creatures to that of our experience as members of a distinctive kind, that is, as rational animals."[10] This human nature—that is, "what is common to us"—does not negate the importance of communal particularities, adds Porter,[11] who explains that the authority of law is identical with the authority of the particular legal system that fundamentally expresses a society's "rationally defendable key values," the "common objects of love" that hold it together.[12]

Thus, Porter is looking for a dynamic model of natural law that leaves a substantial space for social contextuality. In her view, natural morality takes various contextual forms and is therefore never fully expressed by any contextual form. This is a reasonable and attractive framing of natural law theory. However, in order to keep her natural law model "natural," Porter treats the law as an expression of societal identity, depicting society as a space of social harmony, albeit imperfect, rather than an arena for both cooperation and conflict:

> Participation in collaborative activities, in pursuit of shared goals and intentions: these are the hallmarks of properly political relationships, in which men and women jointly pursue aims that are in some sense their own, as well as being shared with others jointly pursuing socially coordinated activities. In this way, the social life natural to us as advanced primates, to which practical reason is naturally receptive, is transformed through the spontaneity of reason into a distinctively political way of life.[13]

Porter offers a variant of natural law theory that can account for cultural pluralism—"distinctive range of alternative ways of living."[14] Additionally, we have seen that her version of natural law retains its critical potential by requiring each community to "rationally defend" its key values. On the one hand, each community has a particular legal system of conventional norms and regulations. On the other hand, a "proper" legal system should be based on rationally defendable principles so as to allow people to question legal regulations when they are unjust.

Porter's moral law is definitely not absolute in the way Kelsen presents the natural law theory. However, an important dimension of morality as a social phenomenon is absent from Porter's theory. This dimension has to do with social and economic conflict. In Porter's view, human beings are rational when they are social, which means that they participate "in the processes through which God providentially governs the world."[15] Porter can account for legitimate differences between communities but has very little to say about social conflict within communities. Naturally, she admits the centrality of community for the law, stating that "it represents a contingent, yet rationally defensible specification of general normative principles justified as such by the foundational authority of the community over its common life."[16] One seeming deficiency in Porter's view of the law is this idea of community as *one* social body held together by a contingent expression of natural values through conventional norms.

The absence of social conflict in Porter's theory of morality and law is related to the positive value ontology and cognitivism that are always incorporated into natural law. The very belief in objective values that can be discovered by human reason contradicts the social fact of persistent value pluralism in one and the same community. While many in Porter's own country would say that the legal system of the United States reflects the true values of democracy and human rights, others have good reasons to claim that its legal system is unjust and legitimizes several forms of injustice. In order to keep these opponents within the discourse on natural morality, Porter needs to group them into one communal body with shared practical rationality. In practice, however, people belong to different social groups, some of which have opposing interests. This defines their practical reasoning in far more fundamental ways than would be the case if a single "community" lay behind the same legal system.

Positive value ontology of the natural law in combination with cognitivism comes with theoretical costs and has political implications. In most cases, natural law theory implies a rejection of value relativism even on the descriptive level. Some theorists, such as Jean Porter, have recognized this challenge and modified the theory in order to account for descriptive value relativism. However, simply acknowledging the existence of reasonable moral disagreements between cultures is not enough. Even when modified, natural law theory lacks a way to explain normative conflicts within a single society. Historically, natural law has been frequently used to present existing legislation as based on "key social values" and therefore as enjoying morally justified authority. Ruling classes, who have used the law in order to maintain their power, invoke moral law to justify this preservation.

Theoretically, natural law can be used by the subjugated to critique positive legislation as a contradiction of moral law. Yet, a more realistic expectation is that those who hold power will successfully present legislation in the service of their own interests as a reflection of true morality. As many critics have demonstrated, natural law tends to legitimize the exclusion of any radical critique of moral and legal conventions on behalf of marginalized groups. If there is a set of true moral values that are reflected in the social conventions of a society, any radical critique of those conventions will necessarily seem unreasonable and/or anti-social.[17]

If I am right, Jean Porter offers a dynamic model of natural law theory that accounts for cultural pluralism while unfortunately downplaying or even hiding the social conflicts that arise whenever democratic struggle for justice becomes possible. Her assertion that societies are united by key values that reflect an eternal moral law rests upon an overly idealistic view of human society. Social conflict constitutes an important political dimension of any society. Justice—moral as well as legal—is therefore marked by these conflicts, and a plausible theory of the dialectics of law, morality, and politics must incorporate this insight.

## NATURAL LAW SECULARIZED

As already mentioned, natural law theory, understood as a theory of moral foundation of valid law, need not be constructed as a theological enterprise. Natural morality that is expected to guide legal practice does not presuppose a belief in God. Nor does it demand a belief in the absolute authority of natural moral law. What it does demand is an endorsement of moral criteria for legally valid norms and the idea that there exists a natural morality beyond its contextual forms. Let us consider some secularized versions of natural law and see whether they can escape the shortcomings of traditional natural law.

Lon L. Fuller presents his theory of the internal morality of law as a variety of natural law that has "nothing to do with any 'brooding omnipresence in the skies'."[18] Fuller defines law as "the enterprise of subjecting human conduct to the governance of rules."[19] This enterprise, in order to function properly, should be conformed to a number of principles internal to the practice of law. Fuller calls them principles of legality, and he views these principles as moral, albeit internally moral. According to Fuller, legal rules should be (1) general, (2) clear, and (3) made known to citizens (promulgated). Legal rules should (4) not be retroactive and (5) not contradict each other. Additionally, legal rules should neither (6) require the impossible nor (7) be changed too often. Finally, (8) there should be congruence between declared legal rules and official actions.[20]

A system of rules that fulfills these eight criteria is described by Fuller as a utopia of legality, and he repeatedly claims that the internal morality of law is one of *aspiration* rather than duty. The internal morality of law guides legal practice but without imposing moral criteria in terms of categorical duties. Thus, in Fuller's version of what he believes is non-religious natural law, the subject of legal activity should aspire to "make the law known, make it coherent and clear, see that your decisions as an official are guided by it, etc."[21]

Fuller's idea—that law, in order to function properly, must (aspire to) fulfill some internal criteria that together constitute legality as the morality of law—is intuitively plausible. Fuller summarizes important insights about factors that obviously affect the functionality or dysfunctionality of legal systems.

However, his thesis that there exists an internal morality of law that is different from substantive moralities (ideas of moral good and moral justice) does not stand up to closer scrutiny. A cogent account of this deficiency in Fuller's position is Hart's critique of the theory of the internal morality of law. First, Hart points to the fact that Fuller does not discriminate between purposive activity—of any kind—and morality. In order to call internal principles of a purposive activity moral, we need to believe that activity in itself constitutes a moral value.[22] Many purposive practices are evil or unjust despite having internal principles of conduct. Describing such principles as internal morality causes more confusion than clarity when we are seeking to scrutinize their practice.

Hart's second objection is related to the first and states that Fuller's principles are ethically neutral: "there is [. . .] no special incompatibility between clear laws and evil."[23] Finally, Hart objects to Fuller's identification of legality with morality. Hart invokes several legal examples (discriminatory regulations in South Africa and Israel, among others) that satisfy the demand of legality while simultaneously violating the demand for moral justice.[24]

Hart is correct in his critique of Fuller's reinterpretation of legality as an "internal morality of law." If morality of law is internal to the practice of legislation and adjudication, it must differ from the morality of other human practices and, most importantly, from morality as the term is normally understood. The ordinary use of "morality" indicates that there is a special dimension of right and wrong, good and evil, in all that human beings do. While particular practices may color what is regarded as just and good, they do not transcend general notions of good and right. When we think of a morally just legal system, we reason in moral terms and discriminate between efficient legal systems on the one hand and just legal systems on the other. In a similar fashion, we can judge a scientific or medical practice in moral or pragmatic terms; we do not normally reduce the former to the latter.

By reducing the morality of law to the internal principles of socially efficient legal practices, Fuller eliminates the very question of how positive law should be related to morality. At most, he discusses the internal virtues of legal practice. His discussion meets with approval from John Finnis, who points out that "[t]he idea of the Rule of Law is based on the notion that a certain quality of interaction between ruler and ruled [. . .] is very valuable for its own sake; it is not merely a means to other social ends. It is not just a 'management technique' in a program of 'social control' or 'social engineering'."[25] However, even Finnis admits that in Fuller's normative theory, "the rule of law does not guarantee every aspect of the common good, and sometimes it does not secure even the substance of the common good."[26]

Although we can reasonably disagree on the issue of whether the rule of law is valuable for its own sake (as in Finnis) or as an instrument for other social ends, it is obvious that Fuller reduces the scope of morality in his theory of the morality of law. What Fuller deliberately leaves aside is the question of the moral justification of substantive legal rules. His theory has nothing to say about the moral quality of legal rules. Therefore, I conclude that Fuller, despite his own aspiration, does not offer a version of natural law theory. Although he addresses the issue of how legal practice should be conducted, the category of "should" in his theory of legality is not a moral concept.

Why is it even important to consider whether Fuller's theory of morality is a form of natural law? Is this not merely an instance of giving labels to theoretical positions, a kind of "internal morality" for ethicists? I believe that Fuller's idea of presenting the internal principles of legal practice as the natural morality of law is not innocent. It borrows from the natural law tradition the idea of having general standards for undertaking a moral scrutiny of conventional norms, but it either reduces morality to a short list of principles or transforms these standards into morally neutral guiding principles. An internal "morality" of this kind cannot claim to be uncovering morally unjust legal conventions.

There are other, more promising attempts to construct a natural law theory beyond its traditional theological framing. In my view, these theories preserve the critical potential of traditional natural law when they incorporate the ideal of respect for human dignity as a categorical principle, that is, as a basic instrument for the moral justification of legal regulations. Let us turn now to a theory of human rights as the protection of human dignity.

## HUMAN DIGNITY AND MORAL RIGHTS IN NON-POSITIVISTIC ACCOUNTS OF MODERN LAW

Christian by origin, human rights can be and often are framed in secular terms. However, when human rights are interpreted as the expression of a "natural morality" that can be grasped by a putatively universal reason, the logic of the Christian tradition of natural law presents itself.

Many would say that this is not a problem: human rights as a form of "basic morality" are still an important correction to the shortcomings of democratic orders in that they protect individuals and minorities from the risks peculiar to majoritarian decision-making. This is how many liberals such as Ronald Dworkin view human rights morality. As is well known, Dworkin regards human rights as a universally valid political morality in that they demand equal respect and concern for all individuals on behalf of the government.[27]

Dworkin further believes that human rights regulations as expressed in the U.S. Constitution are morally justified principles.[28]

Dworkin's theory of human rights is a combination of egalitarian liberalism and the interpretative theory of law. The former is a variant of Rawls's deontological theory of social justice and therefore involves a firm rejection of utilitarianism. The latter is explicitly designed as an alternative to legal positivism, which Dworkin understands as a doctrine that "holds that moral facts cannot figure, at least fundamentally, in the truth conditions of propositions of law."[29] Let us briefly survey Dworkin's political liberalism and his view of law.

Political morality should be a right-based theory, Dworkin believes. He argues that "any right-based theory must presume rights that are not simply the product of deliberate legislation or explicit social custom, but are independent grounds for judging legislation and custom."[30] Thus, rights in Dworkin are moral rights that cannot be reduced to conventionally accepted right claims. Dworkin is critical of legal positivism, which in his view disregards the importance of morality in law and adjudication. However, this does not mean that he straightforwardly defends natural law theory. In Dworkin, human rights have their moral foundation through the rational endorsement of moral equality rather than through the belief in human nature.

Dworkin approves of John Rawls's liberal egalitarianism in which social justice presupposes "a natural right of all men and women to equality of concern and respect."[31] This "natural" morality of equality does not presuppose the existence of God.[32] Nor is it a form of a moral realism. "A natural right to equality" presupposes the ideal of human dignity and political equality as fundamental to practical reason.[33] In other words, a demand for equal concern and respect naturally follows from the proper use of moral reasoning. Moral judgments that discriminate between people with regard to their humanity are simply not fully moral.

According to Dworkin's political ethics, all humans are morally entitled to be treated as equals by the government; social institutions should be scrutinized in light of this moral principle. Human rights, for instance, legitimate claims against the government on behalf of individuals, are the most important instruments for institutional implementation of the basic principle of political morality. Dworkin agrees with Rawls that basic rights should be incorporated into constitutions in order to guide democratic legislation as well as adjudication.

Importantly, human rights in a democracy negate the principle of utility in favor of the principle of equal respect for each and every one: "A right against the Government must be a right to do something even when the majority thinks it would be wrong to do it, and even when the majority would be worse off for having it done."[34]

The institution of law is naturally crucial for implementing the basic right to equal treatment. Simultaneously, this basic moral right, if properly implemented, prevents the law from being "the conqueror's law that dominant class imposes on the weaker, as Marx supposed the law of capitalist society must be."[35] Thus, according to Dworkin, a reasonable theory of political morality must offer a moral reading of constitutional law that secures the efficiency of rights through adjudication and administration.

Turning to the practice of adjudication, Dworkin next develops an alternative to positivism that he calls "interpretative theory of law." The main figure of this theory is the judge who interprets legal regulations by means of the basic principles of political morality. On this reading, Dworkin's near-exclusive focus on adjudication is explained by his conviction that the morality of law is "already" clarified by political ethics. This basic morality transforms lawyers into the main guardians of the moral quality of law. Dworkin is critical of the "political legal positivism" that endorses "a democratic principle: that the people as a whole and not judges, whom the people cannot discharge, should decide what laws should govern them."[36] If Dworkin—here following Rawls—is right that there are basic principles of egalitarian morality that uncorrupted human reason endorses, then an interpretative theory of law is a plausible legal theory. Famously, it requires lawyers to provide the most coherent interpretation of legal propositions in the light of the basic principles of political morality.[37]

Obviously, Dworkin's liberal egalitarianism and his interpretative theory of law have several advantages. One of the most important is the possibility of incorporating minority perspectives—and thus an analysis of power—into the right-based theory of the relationship between morality and positive law. Human rights law, considered as "the majority's promise to minorities"[38] that secures equal respect for each and every person's humanity, is a far more sympathetic interpretation of human rights than the populist vision of human rights as an expression of the traditional values of "the people."[39] As noted in the introduction, human rights law is expected to protect individuals and minorities from abuses of power by the state—a perspective that Dworkin defends.

Additionally, a deontological morality of rights that can be incorporated into a constitution represents a far more promising approach to political ethics than the utilitarian interpretation of rights. We will discuss this in greater detail later on, but Dworkin demonstrates very clearly that the democratic order must be restrained by legally protected rights, interpreted in terms of the principle of equal respect and concern, precisely because majoritarian decisions do not guarantee justice. Obviously, majoritarian decisions tend to override the perspective of minorities and can legitimize different forms of injustice. Dworkin describes his own conception of democracy, what his calls the *constitutional conception of democracy*, as having as its "defining aim [. . .] that collective decisions be made by political institutions whose structure, composition, and practices treat all members of the community, as individuals, with equal concern and respect."[40]

Dworkin is right in claiming that some principles of political morality should be incorporated into the law. As we will see later, the legal positivism discussed and developed in this book endorses this insight of Dworkin's. In a modified version it is compatible with both the separation thesis and non-cognitivism within ethical theory. However, my endorsement of Dworkin's approach to moral rights and his version of non-positivism is tempered by a rejection of the ethical cognitivism that he defends.

Unfortunately, there is no explicitly elaborated ethical theory in Dworkin. As several critics have demonstrated, he uses Rawls's reflective equilibrium when defending the interpretative theory of law. In an analysis of one of Dworkin's earlier articles, Andrei Marmor points to the fact that Dworkin rejects moral realism presupposed by the natural law model of ethical theory. Instead, he embraces a constructivist model and, as quoted by Marmor, Dworkin says that "[I]t demands that we act on principle rather than faith. Its engine is a doctrine of responsibility that requires men to integrate their intuitions and subordinate some of them, when necessary, to that responsibility."[41]

Hence, in Marmor's initiated reading, Dworkin rejects moral realism in favor of Rawlsian constructivism. Simultaneously, Dworkin rejects moral skepticism and defends the *objectivity* of moral judgments, that is, ethical cognitivism. This objectivity is a matter of coherence and holism of moral judgments, the idea in Dworkin that "gives the impression that moral judgments constitute a closed system."[42]

When Dworkin in his later writings describes some legal propositions as being *true* because they flow "from principles of personal and political morality that provide the best interpretation of the other propositions of law generally treated as true," he is in practice constructing a cognitivist position. According to such a position, normative propositions—legal as well as moral—can be either true or false. Although metaphysical objective values do not exist, Dworkin regards the moral principles of the American constitution, when coherently interpreted by the super-rational figure of judge, as true.

In my reading of Dworkin, his cognitivism leaves very little space for alternative approaches to practical reason and hence to political morality as a democratic enterprise. Let us recall Brian Leiter's interpretation of Dworkin's ethical theory. At first glance, this interpretation is nearly opposite to that of Marmor.

In Leiter's view, Dworkin's anti-positivism is in practice an ideological position that legitimizes capitalist social structures. This is so because, according to Leiter, Dworkin's cognitivism implies a moral realism. Explaining the basic constitutional principles of a capitalistic society (here, the United States), Dworkin argues that there exists an objectively correct moral justification for those principles. He thus presents a particular moral position as objectively true, something that disqualifies alternative positions as false. Leiter writes:

> For Dworkin, the idea of the best moral justification of the institutional history of the legal system is a *moral realist* (or *objectivist*) one: Given those principles that explain some significant enough portion of the prior cases, status, administrative rulings, and so on, the one that *really* provides the best moral justification of the legal system is the one that determines what the law is on a particular question—not the one people around happen to *think* provides the best moral justification, but the one that *really does*, even if no one knows it.[43]

Although I am skeptical of Leiter's identification between objectivism and moral realism, he is right when questioning Dworkin's cognitivism. Even when framed as a coherentistic rather than a naturalist position, this cognitivism views moral judgments as objectively true or false. In Dworkin's coherentism, conflicting moral judgments are not related to the perspectives of those who experience one and the same legal order differently.

For a democrat, Dworkin's cognitivism becomes even more problematic when we realize that it is combined with political moralism. Dworkin shares Rawls's view of ethics as a theoretical enterprise that can and should guide political actions, constitutional adjudication included. Their political moralism views politics as a sphere for implementing moral principles that can in turn be exposed by practical reason (here, that of a philosopher who seems to be of the same aristocratic nature as Dworkin's super-judge).

This approach to politics is implausible. Social morality plays a role in the political sphere, but politics is not defined by morality. In Dworkin's case, ethical cognitivism becomes a problem when he tries to grasp the dialectics of politics and morality. Let me explain this point with the help of Herbert Hart's critique of Dworkin's theory of moral rights.

Hart rejects Dworkin's version of deontological theory of rights because he believes that it leads to the conclusion that the substance of moral rights "depend[s] on what external preferences[44] or prejudices are current and likely at any given time in any given society to dominate in a utilitarian decision procedure or majority vote."[45] Hart seems to identify a contradiction in Dworkin's theory of moral rights: on the one hand, there exist moral rights beyond and prior to rights posited by the legislator; on the other hand, the rights of individuals and minorities should protect them from majoritarian external preferences, which means that the content of those moral rights is defined by the preferences that particular majorities happen to hold.

In my reading, Hart recognizes the failure of Dworkin's attempt to combine a theory of moral rights with elements of social constructivism. When Dworkin discusses the content of rights, his position is that of a constructivist: the factual preferences of majorities are fundamental to the social construction of rights. Now, one would not expect such a constructivist to defend ethical cognitivism or to discuss moral propositions as being true or false. If moral rights are basic principles of morality that the uncorrupted reason of the judge should endorse, Dworkin is on shaky ground when he claims that human rights should be defined as the protection of individuals from particular kinds of majoritarian preferences.

However, if we dispense with cognitivism, the claim to legitimacy of protection against majoritarian external preferences on behalf of minorities is perfectly reasonable. Moral rights are legitimate claims. But this legitimacy is not based on some true value judgments exercised by coherent pure reasoning. Rather, moral legitimacy is contextual and political because: (a) to say what proper protection means is to describe a particular social setting in a society; and (b) to demonstrate the legitimacy of moral right claim is a contextual enterprise that demands real communication between political agents. The fact that moral rights are embedded in politics and are socially constructed does not devalue them as moral rights. In practice, this is how Dworkin describes rights in his seminal study *Taking Rights Seriously*. However, he does not reject ethical cognitivism when developing his theory of morality and law further. In Dworkin's ethical theory, moral propositions are either true or false.

If I am right, Dworkin's defense of moral rights and Hart's critique of rights are similar in that both presuppose that a theory of moral rights must include cognitivism. Either there are moral rights that transcend particular social perspectives or there are no moral rights.

In what follows, I will argue that this is a false dilemma. In Dworkin's understanding of rights, the insight that the majoritarian preferences that threaten minorities are crucial to the substance of rights in need of protection, far from being a shortcoming, is a powerful resource. A theory of moral rights that rejects utilitarianism need not be a version of cognitivism. Although Dworkin to some extent realizes this, he still believes that moral rights, in order to exist, need cognitivist justification, that is, to be either verified or falsified.

Additionally, Dworkin's interpretative theory of law suffers from the same weakness as the natural law tradition when its proponents claim that "modern grammar of rights provides a way of expressing virtually all the requirements of practical reasonableness."[46] On one hand, there is a "modern grammar" of rights. On the other hand, this particular grammar is somehow expected to express *everything* that reasonable people have to say. This type of cognitivism is a faulty epistemic position. There are different ways to reason about morality and to construct moral rights. Moreover, this type of cognitivism easily serves the ideological purpose of presenting particular normative perspectives as objectively true. There is no doubt that Dworkin himself is guilty of presenting the American model of human rights as universally valid.

Finally, Dworkin states that moral rights as incorporated into a democratic constitution are instruments for the protection of individuals and minorities. Though progressive in many senses, this belief risks upholding the view that protection against abuses by those in power is the most that the unprivileged can hope for.[47] The notion of human rights as *the* morality of law leaves little room for a democratic critique of the basic structure of the society which that law protects. In Dworkin, this is most obvious when he invests the function of guardian of the political morality of law in the figure of the judge. Those who experience the social structure of their society as deeply unjust are left with only one alternative: to fight for justice as it is stipulated in the [morality of] the constitution. In practice, Dworkin's theory of rights reduces politics to a struggle over the meaning of the constitution. Not only is his theory of law an interpretative theory, his political theory can itself be labeled "interpretative."

Therefore, even Dworkin's theory of basic moral rights involves a significant risk of legitimizing the dominant social order by allowing a "true morality" to limit the political. The conflictual dimension of democratic politics is reduced to the issues of cultural diversity and the constitutional protection of minorities and individuals. Such protection is crucial in all liberal democracies because it constrains majoritarian decision-making and secures the fundamental rights and social status of individuals and minorities. At the same time, however, reducing justice to the legal protection of "natural rights" of individuals and minorities is a way to keep unequal social and economic relations in capitalist society beyond the scope of democratic politics.

Alternative and radical visions of politics and political morality view both rights and other social principles as related to a political struggle and agency on behalf of those whose material conditions make visible the structural injustices of a particular legal and political order. Although the law is always both the instrument and the target of such struggle, a critical approach to the law cannot be reduced to an interpretative practice of adjudication.

## LEGAL POSITIVISM AS A NEGATION OF NATURAL LAW

Legal positivism emerges as a critique of, and alternative to, the natural law approach to the dialectics of law, morality, and politics. From different perspectives, legal positivists question the idea that (a) valid legal regulations must be morally justified, and (b) there exists a natural morality that transcends conventional norms and offers a universal model for justified legal regulations.

In the introduction, I have distanced myself from the legal positivism that regards the question of the moral quality of law as irrelevant to a theory of modern law. By reducing legal positivism to a theory of legal validity, its proponents effectively abandon the most important issue of the relationship between law, morality, and politics—the issue that has been brought into philosophy by natural law and that legal positivism, as an alternative to the natural law tradition, aspires to address more effectively.

There are, however, versions of legal positivism that admit that the very rejection of natural morality is an idea whose moral and political implications must be explicitly addressed. Marxists, feminists, and other radical critics of social injustice invoke this idea in arguing that power structures rather than natural morality should be analyzed by theorists of law engaged in a scrutiny of the moral quality of legal orders. Legal order is a product of social relations, and progressive legal orders can only emerge from a political struggle over concrete material conditions and social relations.[48]

A powerful version of this kind of positivism is Axel Hägerström's understanding of the relationship between law, politics, and morality. Following Karl Marx in his critique of Hegelian idealism, Hägerström views law, morality, and religion as secondary to the material interests of social classes. The dominant class tends to present the legal regulations of the society as the expression of natural morality rather than as a matter of human choices. Rejecting this claim is essential for all those who are struggling to improve their social conditions. In practice, Hägerström notes, every social class has its own morality.[49]

Thus, anyone who succeeds in representing their own social class's morality as "natural" has acquired a powerful political and legal instrument. Hägerström uses Marx's understanding of proletarian morality as an example of the instrumental representation[50] of a particular morality as "natural." According to Hägerström, the idea of the morality of the proletariat, as an expression of Marx's own personal "deep emotion in regard to suffering of the inferior class," demands that the proletariat organize itself and fulfill its historical mission [to put an end to class society].[51] This "historical mission" allows Marx to represent the moral ideal of social solidarity and self-sacrifice for the sake of one's class (in capitalist society, the proletariat) as natural and pre-given by the course of history. Marx rejects Hegel's idealistic metaphysics of history precisely in order to reveal natural morality as the incarnation of the objective development of social relations of production. A scientific enterprise of historical materialism describes this "objective" development and metaphysics reappears in Marxian thought.

Hägerström offers an elegant critique of the ideological component in Marx's representation of proletarian morality as a description of social development according to objective historical laws. Fundamental to this critique is Hägerström's belief that social scientists must firmly reject metaphysics. He constructs his own value nihilism as a radical critique of positive value ontology, even when such an ontology is an element of Marxism.

Let us recall the main content of Hägerström's value nihilism. On the theoretical level, Hägerström questions economic determinism and argues that understanding the law, like morality, requires more than an explanation of how they are related to social relations of production. Hägerström sees emotivism as a revisioning of the Marxian understanding of morality as the protection of economic interests. In Marx, material interests upon which the proletarian morality is based are progressive when they become an instrument of the objective historical telos (a communist society). According to emotivism, moral judgments are expressions of emotions, and Marx's own strongly emotional attitude toward the suffering of proletariat accounts for his depiction of social solidarity as the morality of a historical mission. In the final paragraph of Hägerström's essay on social teleology in Marxism, we read: "Marx himself is an example of the banal psychological experience that human beings tend to construct the reality according to their own wishes."[52] As I see it, Hägerström agrees with Marx that morality (like law and religion) is secondary to material positions but questions the naturalism of economic determinism and introduces emotions as a defining element of moral evaluation.

Objective values do not simply exist, awaiting discovery by reason. Rather, moral judgments express human emotions. These emotions are related to the fundamental interests of human beings—interests that are defined by their social conditions. For the most part, Hägerström uses "emotions" (*känslor*) and "interests" (*intressen*) interchangeably. In the essay entitled "Social Justice," we read: "Thus, the ideas about justice and injustice are defined by our emotions. What is just for one class because it correlates to its interests is unjust for another class because it contradicts its interests."[53] Hägerström goes on to claim that the fact that justice and injustice of social conditions are defined by "initial interests or emotions" does not devalue the importance of moral ideas. Rather, as he understands it, value nihilism is itself a radical expression of *moral* autonomy:

> The feeling of guilt and responsibility in relation to the demands of the absolute will must melt away. A genuinely autonomous morality is here, defined entirely by immediate love of what we evaluate most of all. [. . . Human being's] fear [not to fulfil moral demands] shall be entirely directed to her own highest values, relative realization of which alone makes her life worth to live.[54]

Thus, Hägerström's value nihilism includes an important normative component, namely an ideal of emancipation which presupposes that whenever we endorse the existence of objective moral values, and hence moral truth, we give up on freedom.

In terms of metaethics, Hägerström defends a non-cognitivism that firmly rejects the idea that moral judgments can be described as either true or false. In the absence of objective values, our moral judgments should be understood as expressions of emotions (equated with interests). An important practical advantage of this position, according to Hägerström, is that it counteracts the fanaticism inspired by a belief in one's own moral ideas as expressions of true values.[55]

Hägerström's critique of positive value ontology and ethical cognitivism is decisive for his particular form of legal positivism. This positivism is not just a theory of the criteria of valid positive law. Instead, it is a theory that seeks to overcome the idealistic heritage of the natural law tradition as preserved in the modern theory of law, Marxian included. Whenever a scholar presents man-made constructions as objectively given, she misinterprets social reality and risks producing ideology rather than social science.

Hägerström is only right up to a point. The weakness of his theory of morality and law lies in his belief that we have to choose between either moral realism coupled with cognitivism or value nihilism that rejects the very project of scrutinizing social regulations rationally. Hägerström does not even consider a possibility of undertaking a rational scrutiny of moral conventions beyond the paradigm of moral realism and cognitivism. In his essay "Scandinavian Realism," Hart rightly points to this particular dogmatic aspect of the heritage from Hägerström, which he describes as "the peculiar dogmatic insistence [. . .] that if a statement cannot be analysed as a statement of fact or expression of feeling it *must* be 'metaphysical'."[56]

By excluding the very possibility of a rational scrutiny of morality beyond metaphysics, Hägerström reduces the ethicist's task to a study of "factual evaluations in their historical contexts."[57] Although he starts with a most important and morally loaded critique of the metaphysics of natural morality, he ends up by aborting the very project of undertaking a rational critique of the moral quality of social conventions.

As Richard Hare has demonstrated, there exists another version of ethical theory, one that combines negative value ontology with an endorsement of the possibility of making a rational critique of moral judgments. Hare's prescriptivism claims that the main function of moral judgment is practical, namely commendatory. In order to be valid, moral prescriptions must be universalizable. As Hare writes:

> Universalizability can be explained in various equivalent ways; it comes to this, that if we make different moral judgements about situations which we admit to be identical in their universal descriptive properties, we contradict ourselves.[58]

Hare's version of ethical theory preserves the critical mode of natural law by seeking the instruments of a rational moral critique of positive regulations. Simultaneously, it rejects any form of pre-given morality that a theorist might describe as true.

My aim in what follows is to further develop a constructivist account of morality that allows for a rational normative critique of social conventions. I will demonstrate how such a theory can improve the theoretical quality and critical potential of a legal positivism that takes the question of moral quality of legal regulations seriously. I will start by interpreting three forms of such a positivism in order to show how, potent as they are, each contains room for improvement.

## NOTES

1. This did not stop Kelsen from engaging in the metaethical discussions. See for example Torben Spaak, "Kelsen's Metaethics," *Ratio Juris* 35, no. 2 (2022): 97–244. Kelsen's legal positivism is tied to a particular interpretation of moral relativism as a precondition for reliable moral scrutiny of conventions. This interpretation—and not his concept of law—explains why Kelsen believes that moral justification of social norms is beyond the scope of scientific analysis.

2. Hans Kelsen, *Pure Theory of Law* (Clark, NJ: The Lawbook Exchange, Ltd, Clark, 2002), 68–69.

3. Hans Kelsen, *General Theory of Law and State* (Clark, NJ: The Lawbook Exchange, 2009), 394.

4. Most importantly, traditional Islamic and Jewish approaches to law do not discriminate between law and morality in the same way Christian traditions do. Divine law is given by God to human beings and the meaning of that law cannot but be co-created by human beings. Reason is a source for interpretations, but this reason is not the univocal reason of the Christian tradition of natural law. See, for example, Mohammad Hashim Kamali, *Shari'ah Law. An Introduction* (Oxford: Oneworld, 2008), 99–122; 162–178. Francois-Xavier Licari, *An Introduction to Jewish Law* (Cambridge, UK: Cambridge University Press, 2019).

5. Both Jean Porter and John Finnis have demonstrated that Kelsen, Hart, and Raz wrongly accused natural law theory of identification between legal validity and moral justification. The very discrimination between posited norms and morally justified norms is a crucial part of the classic natural law. See for example John Finnis, *Natural Law and Natural Rights."* Second Edition (Oxford, UK: Oxford University Press, 2011), 25–27.

6. Jean Porter, *Ministers of the Law. A Natural Law Theory of Legal Authority* (Cambridge, UK: William B. Eerdmans Publishing Company, 2010), 243. My emphasis.

7. Jean Porter, *Nature as Reason. A Thomistic Theory of the Natural Law* (Cambridge, UK: William B. Eerdmans Publishing Company, 2005), 13–14.

8. Ibid., 16.

9. See, for example, William Schweiker, *Theological Ethics and Global Dynamics* (Hoboken, NJ: Wiley-Blackwell, 2004).

10. Porter, *Ministers of the Law,* 102.

11. Ibid., 108.

12. Ibid., 244–245.

13. Ibid., 106.

14. Ibid., 107.

15. Ibid., 89–90.

16. Ibid., 235.

17. See, for example, Gianni Vattimo, *Nihilism and Emancipation. Ethics, Politics, and Law* (New York: Columbia University Press, 2007).

18. Lon L. Fuller, *The Morality of Law.* Revised edition (New Haven, CT: Yale University Press, 1969), 96.

19. Ibid., 96.

20. Ibid., 46–90.

21. Ibid., 42.

22. Herbert L. A. Hart, *Essays in Jurisprudence and Philosophy* (Oxford, UK: Clarendon Press, 1983), 350.

23. Ibid., 352.

24. Ibid., 352.

25. Finnis, *Natural Law and Natural Rights*, 274.

26. Ibid., 274.

27. Ronald Dworkin, *Taking Rights Seriously* (Cambridge, MA: Harvard University Press, 1977), 180–183.

28. Ronald Dworkin, *Justice in Robes* (Cambridge, Massachusetts: Harvard University Press, 2006), 28–30. Ronald Dworkin, *Freedom's Law. The Moral Reading of the American Constitution* (Cambridge, MA: Harvard University Press, 1996), 2–12.

29. Dworkin, *Justice in Robes*, 26.

30. Dworkin, *Taking Rights Seriously*, 177.

31. Ibid., 182.

32. As already mentioned, according to Christian traditions all humans are created in the image of God and therefore to violate humanity is to violate God. In Islam, the reasoning is different and straightforward political. God is regarded to be the only one whom human beings should subjugate themselves to. Any time a human being expects others to subjugate themselves to her a sin against God is committed.

33. Dworkin, *Taking Rights Seriously*, 198–199.

34. Ibid., 194.

35. Ibid., 204.

36. Dworkin, *Justice in Robes*, 27.

37. Ibid., 14.
38. Dworkin, *Taking Rights Seriously*, 205.
39. On traditionalist approaches to human rights see for example Elena Namli, "Christianity and Human Rights Law. Orthodox Perspectives," in *Christianity and International Law. An Introduction*, eds. Pamela Slotte and John D. Haskell (Cambridge, UK: Cambridge University Press, 2021), 317–336.
40. Dworkin, *Freedom's Law*, 17.
41. Andrei Marmor, "Holism, and Interpretation: The Epistemic Foundations of Dworkin's Legal Theory," *Law and Philosophy* 10, no. 4 (1991): 390.
42. Ibid., 407.
43. Brian Leiter, "Marx, Law, Ideology, Legal Positivism," *Virginia Law Review* 101, no. 4 (2005): 1191.
44. External preferences are "preferences for the assignment of goods and opportunities to others." Dworkin, *Taking Rights Seriously*, 234.
45. Herbert L. A. Hart, *Essays in Jurisprudence and Philosophy* (Oxford, UK: Clarendon Press, 1983), 213.
46. Finnis, *Natural Law and Natural Rights*, 198.
47. For critique of human rights as ideology see for example Christoph Menke, *Critique of Rights* (Cambridge, UK: Polity, 2020).
48. Axel Hägerström, *Inquiries into the Nature of Law and Morals* (Stockholm: Almqvist och Wiksell, 1953).
49. Axel Hägerström, *Social teleologi i marxismen* (Uppsala: Akademiska Bokhandeln, 1909), 59.
50. Obviously, Hägerström was one of the earliest critics of Marxism as an ideology production. This critique was not a rejection of political pragmatism on behalf of Marxists, but a rejection of the representation of political ideals as scientific. In his own version of Marxism, Hägerström seeks to discriminate between scientific analysis on one hand and political program on the other.
51. Hägerström, *Social teleologi i marxismen*, 68–69. My translation.
52. Ibid., 69. My translation.
53. Axel Hägerström, *Socialfilosofiska uppsatser* (Stockholm: Bonniers, 1966), 109. My translation.
54. Ibid., 53. My translation.
55. Ibid., 54.
56. Hart, *Essays in Jurisprudence and Philosophy*, 164.
57. Hägerström, *Socialfilosofiska uppsatser*, 56.
58. Richard M. Hare, *Moral Thinking. Its Levels, Method and Point* (Oxford, UK: Clarendon Press, 1981), 21.

# *Chapter 3*

# H. L. A. Hart

## *Utilitarian Ethics and Democratic Law*

Herbert Hart (1907–1992) was, and in many regards remains, the most influential theorist of law in Anglo-Saxon philosophy since the Second World War. He entered the debate on the relationship between law and morality in the late 1950s. At that time, dissatisfaction with classical German legal positivism had created the political and academic conditions for a resurgence in the belief that moral criteria can and should be incorporated into the concept of law. Rejecting this view, Hart offers a sophisticated, although admirably clear, theory of law that views law and morality as analytically and socially distinct. Simultaneously, he argues that developing a moral critique of law is a philosophical task of paramount political importance, something to which he himself has made a substantial contribution. For this very reason, Hart's version of legal positivism is significant for this study.

In this chapter, I offer a reconstruction and critique of Hart's understanding of the relationship between law, morality, and politics. I begin with a short summary of Hart's understanding of the concept of law before moving on to his discussion of law and morality. Here, it will be demonstrated that a balanced interpretation of Hart demands the recognition of his distinction between critical and positive morality. This distinction is crucial for Hart's thesis that moral critique of law is a political resource, especially in a democracy. I argue that both Hart's positivism and his critique of natural rights should be interpreted in terms of social constructivism, the most politically progressive epistemology of both law and morality. For this reason, Hart's legal positivism is not a legitimization of the moral conformism of *Gesetz als Gesetz* but a form of legal positivism that can inspire a philosophical and political critique of unjust law.

I then proceed by challenging Hart's understanding of democratic politics and his utilitarianism. Although Hart legitimately and consistently endorses liberal democracy's moral pluralism, there are problematic aspects to the reduction of morally and politically unjust domination to direct coercion that is part of his defense of liberalism. In my view, it suffers from a failure to recognize the social position of individuals and groups with regard to power. Hart offers a valuable examination of differences in "moral opinion" on matters of private and sexual morality, but he overlooks a number of areas of disagreement on matters of social justice. The distribution of economic, political, and discursive resources and power is regulated by law, which makes disagreement about morally justified distribution a central element of any plausible theory of law, morality, and politics.

Hart's endorsement of utilitarianism is closely linked to his liberalism and view of politically and morally relevant issues. In what follows, I argue that we can reconstruct several valuable tools for a critique of natural law and natural rights from Hart's distinction between conventional and critical morality. This critique is not determined by Hart's defense of utilitarian normative theory but operates on a metaethical level. Therefore, I further develop it as a form of ethical constructivism. Most importantly, I suggest that the charge of fundamentalism and conservatism that is a crucial component of Hart's critique of right-based political ethics does not apply to a constructivist and deontological theory of rights.

## THE LAW: CONCEPT AND SCOPE

Hart's version of positivism is a late, post-Second World War version of legal positivism, a version that relates to previous forms of legal positivism as well as developments within the tradition of natural law. Hart formulates his version of the separation thesis as follows: "we shall take Legal Positivism to mean the simple contention that it is in no sense a necessary truth that laws reproduce or satisfy certain demands of morality, though in fact they have often done so."[1] As Hart explicitly states, his theory provides "an improved analysis of the distinctive structure of a municipal legal system and a better understanding of the resemblances and differences between law, coercion, and morality, as types of social phenomena."[2] This statement is significant for any plausible interpretation of Hart. Hart's inquiry focuses on three aspects. First, the relationship between law and morality as two different albeit related *social phenomena.* Second, the relationship between law, morality, and different types of coercion. Third, the legal system of a nation-state as a model of *law*.

For the purposes of my analysis, it is important that Hart does not identify the relationship between law and politics as a specific objective of his theory. Even so, I argue that there is a political dimension to Hart's legal positivism

My aim is to explicate this dimension and scrutinize its role for Hart's theory of law and morality.

Let us recapitulate the most important components of Hart's legal positivism, his view of law and his understanding of the similarities and differences between law and morality. Hart aims to offer a theory of law that grasps some (but not all) of the central features of law. This theory seeks to avoid the simplification of reducing law to "an order backed by threats" or treating "the complex idea" of morality as its necessary component.[3]

According to Hart, law is a system of rules. It is a union of primary rules of obligation with secondary rules, for instance, rules that define how to identify and change valid (primary) legal rules. Whereas the primary rules are concerned with what subjects of law must or must not do, the secondary rules "specify the ways in which the primary rules may be conclusively ascertained, introduced, varied, and the fact of their violation conclusively determined."[4] "Rule of recognition" is Hart's famous term for the conventional rules that vary between societies but whose function is to identify the primary rules of obligation in a conclusive manner.

It is crucial that this conceptualization presupposes what Hart calls the internal point of view, "the view of those who [. . .] *use* the rules as standards for the appraisal of their own and others' behaviour."[5] There is, of course, a logical link between this internal perspective and Hart's belief that rules of *obligation* are the core of any legal system. Hart disagrees with John Austin, who famously connects the authority of law to binding commands. He also rejects the idea, shared by Hans Kelsen among others, that sanctions are crucial to the existence of legal norms. Hart believes that sanctions have two important albeit inessential functions within legal orders. First, they guarantee that "those who voluntary obey [the law] shall not be sacrificed to those who would not."[6] Second, sanctions are centrally important for the control of dominated groups whose only motive for obedience is threat.[7] Hart therefore seems to believe that direct domination is not essential for stable social relations and therefore for the law. Like morality, law is basically a system of rules of obligation that makes it possible for humans to peacefully coexist and cooperate within a given society. Hart even represents a legal system to which subjects regard themselves morally bound as highly stable.[8] However, belief in morally justified law is not necessary for the very existence of legal systems.

Hart offers a conceptualization of the legal system by specifying two necessary and sufficient social conditions of its existence. The first is that primary rules must be generally obeyed and the second is that "its rules of recognition specifying the criteria of legal validity and its rules of change and adjudication must be effectively accepted as common public standards of official behaviour by its officials."[9] Hart sees legal rules as similar to the rules of games: for each to function properly, it must be intelligible and something that most people are able to obey. Additionally, they must not be retrospective.[10]

As further clarification of his concept of law, Hart describes the similarities as well as the differences between law and morality. A number of fundamental similarities between law and (conventional) morality are listed in *The Concept of Law*. Both social phenomena are binding in ways that are independent of individual consent. Both are supported by considerable social pressure—compliance with law and morality is not regarded as a matter of praise. Both include rules governing socially important situations. Finally, both make "demands which must obviously be satisfied by any group of human beings who are to succeed in living together."[11] Hart then proceeds by identifying four formal features of morality that distinguish it from legal and other social rules. First, any moral rule is essentially regarded by a society as something of great importance. Such social recognition of importance is not essential to all legal rules, according to Hart.[12] Driving on the left side of the road and other legal rules of this stripe are of no moral importance in the sense that they are not "preferable to alternatives." Similarly, it makes no difference to a person's sense of moral guilt whether their broken promise has been witnessed by one witness or two. Particular legal rules for how to witness a promise are morally neutral.[13]

Second, moral rules are immune from deliberate change. While new legal rules can be intentionally and immediately introduced by the legislator, moral rules are not the product of deliberate human choices.[14] Third, moral blame always presupposes the voluntary character of a moral offence. Legal blame "is not excluded by the demonstration that an accused person could not have kept the law."[15] Finally, social moral pressure appeals to one's conscience, to the very moral status of broken rules.[16]

These formal features are fundamental for conventional moral rules as Hart understands them. In *The Concept of Law*, he admits that, alongside the moral conventions of a given society, there exist moral ideals of different kind, namely an "enlightened or true morality," a concept that seems to correspond to that of "critical morality" in his other writings.[17] Although these two kinds of morality can and should be used in order to critically approach existing legal rules, legal validity is not identical with compliance with moral criteria.

To sum up, Hart's concept of law makes a firm distinction between the validity of legal rules and their morality. Legal validity is defined by the rule of recognition, which is always a set of conventional rules of identification, change, and adjudication. The content of primary legal rules of obligation may have or have no moral importance. If it does, a legal rule may be described as immoral, which does not change its status as valid law. Although Hart may be arguing that particular rules of law may conflict with morality, he believes that "the [legal] system as a whole must rest on a generally diffused conviction that there is a moral obligation to obey its rules."[18] This "diffuse conviction" is of sociological interest because it affects the functioning of legal systems. However, it does not constitute a moral obligation.

While the rules of recognition differ between cultures, even an external observer can identify them precisely as secondary rules of recognition. Ultimately and most importantly, Hart views rules of recognition as the products of the social structures of concrete societies. Contextual social practices constitute different rules of recognition and such rules may or may not include moral criteria. Hart's endorsement of the plurality of rules of recognition is explicit in his comments on Ronald Dworkin's critique of his legal theory. Hart views Dworkin's interpretative theory of law as a theory of adjudication in a specific legal culture with a particular rule of recognition.[19] According to Hart, there is no contradiction between his own general theory and the fact that in some legal systems, such as the American constitutionalism defended by Dworkin, moral principles can be part of the rule of recognition. This is one of the reasons why Hart accepts the term "soft positivism" as a label for his own position.[20]

Although Hart's positivist general theory of law does not focus on the process of adjudication, it squarely includes adjudication as an important dimension of the law. Hart famously admits that judges in many cases necessarily legislate and that this necessity is related to what he calls "penumbra of uncertainty." He reminds us that John Austin himself characterized the view of complete separation of powers as "childish fiction."[21] A proper application of the general rule in the process of adjudication demands some identified *social aims* that control adjudication.[22] However, it is essential that social aims are conventional aims in both a moral and a non-moral sense: they do not—at least, not necessarily—comply with the morally justified principles that Hart positions within the critical level of morality. Herein, lies the main difference between Hart and one of his most notorious critics, Dworkin. While Dworkin interprets catalogs of rights such as the U.S. Constitution as expressions of objective moral principles that should guide the true adjudication,[23] Hart understands any normativity as fundamentally conventional, that is, as constructed by means of concrete social structures and cultures. In the opening section of *The Concept of Law*, Hart repeats Austin's statement that "[c]onstitutional law is positive morality merely,"[24] and it is clear that Hart shares this belief with Austin. Moreover, Hart insists that we should not view law as if it were all penumbra. Even in this regard, Hart's position on adjudication is diametrically opposite to Dworkin's. While Dworkin, almost exclusively, pays attention to hard cases, Hart is interested in ordinary legal practice.

Thus, in my view the controversy between Hart and Dworkin demonstrates very clearly that Hart's positivism is not a rejection of moral critique of law. Rather, it is a rejection of the claim that legal validity presupposes the moral legitimacy of legal rules. We now turn to the political implications of such a rejection.

## LEGALITY, MORALITY, AND POLITICS

Hart's defense of legal positivism includes politically and morally normative components. In his Oliver Wendell Holmes Lecture at the Harvard Law School, delivered in April 1957, Hart credits the utilitarianism of Austin and Bentham for its ability to combine "the passion for reform with respect for law together with a due recognition of the need to control the abuse of power even when power is in the hands of reformers."[25] Moreover, he views this utilitarianism as "the vanguard of a movement which labored with passionate intensity and much success to bring about a better society and better laws."[26] Hart insists that in order to understand Austin's and Bentham's legal positivism, that is, the firm separation between law as it is and law as it ought to be, we need to start by recognizing positivism's relation to the progressive political mission of utilitarianism. Hart believes that Bentham's utilitarianism in particular greatly contributed toward the ending of slavery and the advancement of liberalism and democracy in general.

Hart takes ideas from classical utilitarianism and frequently draws on the distinction between positive morality and critical morality.[27] In his Harry Camp Lecture on "The Legal Enforcement of Morality," he discriminates between "'positive morality,' the morality actually accepted and shared by a given social group" and critical morality as "the general moral principles used in the criticism of social institutions including positive morality."[28] As already noted, it is of crucial importance for any plausible interpretation of Hart's positivism to recognize this distinction between conventional and critical morality. Although Hart rejects the moral realism of natural law and natural rights,[29] he does endorse the possibility of making a rational critique of moral conventions.

Thus, Hart views the utilitarianism of Austin, Bentham, and Mill as the best normative theory for a critique of moral conventions. Deontological normative theory, according to Hart, tends to include a metaphysics of pregiven morality and therefore to become dogmatic. This dogmatism implies the existence of fundamental moral values beyond social critique. Hart seems to believe that utilitarianism, unlike deontological theory, is immune to dogmatism because it does not presuppose moral realism. He regards utilitarianism as a type of critical morality that does not demand any metaphysics.

Therefore, it should be used in order to question bad laws, but it cannot be used to make dogmatic claims about right and wrong.

As I see it, Hart treats utilitarianism as *the* only way to achieve a non-fundamentalist critical morality beyond the moral conventions of a given society. Additionally, Bentham's legal positivism in combination with utilitarianism offers a middle way between anarchism and quietism. The firm separation between law as it is and law as it ought to be helps "to steer [between] the danger that law and its authority may be dissolved in man's conceptions of what law ought to be and the danger that the existing law may supplant morality as a final test of conduct and so escape criticism."[30]

The quotation above clearly demonstrates that Hart endorses morality, not law, as a means of social critique and thus political transformation. The "morality" here corresponds to critical moral reasoning. In its function, it is similar to how practical reason is understood by the tradition of natural law: it can and should challenge conventionally accepted injustices. Yet, Hart rejects the very idea of human nature or some kind of objective moral principle as the criterion of scrutiny for positive law. In "Social Solidarity and the Enforcement of Morality," he rejects the view of morality as "a uniquely true or correct set of principles—not man-made, but either awaiting man's discovery by the use of reason or (in a theological setting) awaiting its disclosure by revelation."[31] The challenge is thus to offer a normative theory that can be used as a critique of law while simultaneously not presupposing moral realism on the metaethical level.

Before we take a closer look at how Hart deals with this challenge, some further remarks are in order about Hart's understanding of the relationship between law, morality, and politics. As I see it, the most radical component of Hart's legal theory is precisely his claim that social and political injustice cannot be dealt with by means of a moral interpretation of law *within the legal domain*. In order to deal with unjust law, we should start by admitting the existence of unjust laws. Unjust laws are still laws, and we, as citizens, need to approach them by means of moral evaluation if we are to challenge the demand to obey legally valid rules.

Responding to the critique of legal positivism as developed by Gustav Radbruch, Hart states that resistance to unjust laws is morally based. Yet, such resistance implies disobedience to unjust laws, not the claim that these laws are not laws. As is well known, Radbruch's personal experiences of support for Nazi regime framed by the legal culture of *Gesetz als Gesetz* led him to conclude that legal positivism should be abandoned. Lawyers can and should declare clearly unjust laws to be invalid and, in so doing, make a defense of legality and the rule of law. Hart accuses Radbruch of "an enormous overvaluation of the importance of the bare fact that a rule may be said to be a valid rule of law, as if this, once declared, was conclusive of the final moral question: 'Ought this rule of law be obeyed?'."[32] Hart's polemics against Radbruch make clear that his defense of legal positivism is based on the distinction between recognizing a rule as a valid law and recognizing the *moral* duty to obey such a rule. Proving that a particular rule is a law is not the same as proving we have a moral duty to obey it.[33] In the next step, Hart argues that utilitarianism, if combined with a positivistic account of legal validity, offers an efficient tool for mobilizing against evil laws. For Hart, the idea that unjust laws are simply not laws is counterintuitive.

Another important insight, which Hart presents in the context of a critique of Radbruch, is that the natural law approach risks obscuring the genuine "moral quandary" that we confront in unjust laws. Hart discusses the case of a German woman who, in order to get rid of her husband, had denounced him to the Nazi authorities, an action she later defended on the grounds that it was lawful according to the laws of Nazi Germany. Hart is critical of the ruling of a postwar German court that followed Radbruch, who had stated that "every lawyer and judge should denounce statutes that transgressed the fundamental principles not as merely immoral but as having no legal character."[34] The court pronounced the legal statutes to be invalid because it found them "contrary to the sound conscience and sense of justice of all decent human beings."[35] According to Hart, such a decision conceals that the real choice of the court was to choose the lesser of two evils, for instance, either to let the woman go unpunished or to sentence her under a retrospective law.[36]

At issue here is the genuine moral dilemma confronted by lawyers when dealing with unjust laws. The dilemma demands institutional, political approaches and therefore cannot be resolved by means of "theoretical speculation" on behalf of the lawyer. Unjust laws create moral dilemmas for individuals, but to resolve them we need political changes rather than judicial efforts. Therefore, in practice, Hart accuses Radbruch of offering an apolitical speculation in matters that cannot be but politically resolved.

Unjust valid statutes are laws, for which reason critical morality demands institutional and political changes rather than the exercise of moral reason on the part of a judge. Additionally and importantly, Hart is aware of moral pluralism that cannot be eliminated by such a reason and therefore demands moral choice. As he states in *The Concept of Law*, "[j]udicial decision [. . .] often involves a choice between moral values, and not merely the application of some single outstanding moral principle; for it is folly to believe that where the meaning of the law is in doubt, morality always has a clear answer to offer."[37]

Let us summarize the most important elements of Hart's view of law, morality, and politics. Hart understands the law as obviously connected to both morality and politics, but it is not the case that law, for being a valid law, must comply with some universal moral standards. Bad and even evil law exist and the only way to begin to improve them is to admit their existence as morally unjust laws. Hart here invokes the distinction between conventional morality (positive morality) and critical morality. Conventional morality is naturally incorporated into legislation, while critical morality is a tool for critique of it. As Neil MacCormick has rightly observed, "Hart was a positivist because he was a critical moralist."[38]

Hart insists that utilitarianism is the best way to answer the *moral* question of whether particular laws ought to be obeyed. The issue at hand is how to evaluate laws morally. In my reading of Hart, there is a profoundly democratic aspect to this question that makes utilitarianism attractive for him, namely the fact that the highly concrete, material interests of different people and real social conflicts can be incorporated into a normative theory that offers rational justificatory tools.

## WHY UTILITARIANISM?

Let us look more closely at Hart's use and defense of utilitarianism, something that is of crucial importance for this study precisely because Hart viewed utilitarianism as the most plausible approach to political morality and therefore the most reasonable way to limit the power of the state and justify the use of power. Hart wrote about utilitarianism just prior to an important paradigm shift in political ethics: the return of deontological ethics and the theory of moral rights in the wake of John Rawls's *A Theory of Justice*, which rendered invalid the traditional utilitarian skepticism toward basic rights. Importantly, Hart did not change his mind and remained loyal to utilitarianism, which he presented as the most progressive normative theory.

Hart is critical of right-based normative theory because it has not yet solved, and perhaps cannot solve, the problem of how to prioritize rights understood as justified claims on behalf of persons. Hart believes that modern theories of moral rights share with the doctrine of natural rights the philosophical sin of "criterionlessness." Hart writes that Bentham himself made "the most serious charge, namely that of 'criterionlessness' [. . .] against the doctrine of natural rights and to which contemporary philosophers who have opposed to utilitarianism right-based political and moral theories are still struggling to find answer."[39]

My own view is that this criterionlessness is connected with the dilemma faced by all deontological theories of rights: whether to present a short list of basic rights and justify such a reduction, or to present a more ambitious list of rights supported by a guiding principle of prioritization. Hart discusses two ideologically opposite forms of the theory of rights: one from the

Conservative Right as defended by Robert Nozick; and one from the Liberal Left in the figures of Rawls and Dworkin.

The first is grounded in the idea of the moral importance of the distinctness of individual humans, something that Nozick believes is overlooked by the utilitarian ethics. In an article entitled "Between Utility and Rights," Hart presents Nozick's arguments against utilitarianism and admits that they in fact challenge the utilitarian philosopher. However, Nozick does not offer any convincing justification for his own particular list of moral rights: "why should rights be limited as they are by Nozick to what Bentham called the negative services to others, that is to abstention from such things as murder, assault, theft, and breach of contract?"[40] Hart rightly points out that other claims on behalf of humans (for social rights, for example) could be regarded as justified and thus as being moral rights. In my reading, Hart's main theoretical[41] criticism of Nozick is that he reduces rights to a short list of negative freedoms in order to avoid the issue of prioritizing between conflicting rights, a thorny issue for any theory of rights. Put differently, when Nozick prioritizes the value of negative freedom above other values, he is effectively concealing the implicitly dogmatic basis of his political ethics.

Dworkin's essentially Rawlsian theory of rights postulates that entitlement to equal concern and respect is central to political morality. Although Hart endorses egalitarian morality in utilitarian terms (each person to count for one, nobody for more than one), he believes that egalitarianism, if expressed by the principle of equal concern and respect, tends to present a particular understanding of equality as fundamental that closely resembles a metaphysics of natural law. In Hart's view, for a theory of rights to be convincing it should be based on "seemingly uncontroversial ideas." Nozick's understanding of freedom and Dworkin's view on equality do not fulfill this criterion.[42]

How, then, should we evaluate Hart's critique of normative theory of basic rights? I believe Hart is right to remain critical of Nozick's and Dworkin's models of normative ethics because they include strong assumptions about human beings and societies. Those assumptions remind us of realism of natural law in that they are expected to transcend normative disagreements. In fact, normative theory of rights often presupposes both naturalism and cognitivism at a metaethical level. For example, Ronald Dworkin believes that the principles of human rights as stipulated in the U.S. Constitution are *objectively* right ("true" in the terminology of his response to the Hart's postscript).

In opposition to Dworkin, Hart defends a non-cognitivism which demonstrates that value judgments, moral as well as legal and political, are embedded in social relations. Whereas Dworkin uses his theory of rights to identify "true propositions of law," Hart uses the term "valid" in relation to law, for the most part avoiding any claim to objectivity within morality. As noted earlier, Hart depicts moral principles, even on a critical level, as the instruments of a social critique of concrete and relevant injustices rather than as objective or universal. All principles and norms are related to the interests of concrete people in particular societies.[43] Hart's normative position is therefore not, *pace* Dworkin, an act of Archimedean distancing by an Oxford professor.[44] Rather, it is a political stance against moral fundamentalism, liberal fundamentalism included, and in defense of moral pluralism and liberal democracy.[45]

People disagree on moral and political matters and these disagreements cannot be resolved by recourse to some kind of objective universal morality. This is so because we are social beings with particular and different interests. We can agree on that. Yet, Hart's interpretation of the theory of rights is anything but generous. To my knowledge, he has never considered the possibility of a theory of rights that does not include strong assumptions about freedom, equality, or human nature. In fact, Hart identifies an element in Dworkin's theory of moral rights that clearly depicts basic rights in a non-cognitivist manner. As Hart notes, Dworkin eventually defines human rights (moral rights) as rights that "are in danger of being overridden by the corrupting element" of majoritarian decision procedures or utilitarian arguments.[46] Hart's objection to this interpretation of the main function of moral rights is surprising: "What moral rights we have will, on this view, depend on what external preferences or prejudices are current and likely at any given time in any given society to dominate in a utilitarian decision procedure of majority vote."[47]

Precisely here, in Dworkin's discussion of human rights as a protection against majoritarian conventions, we discern the possibility of justifying moral rights in a way that demands neither metaphysical foundations nor cognitivism. Although Hart sees a potential contradiction in the theory of rights as presented by Dworkin, he cannot imagine a theory of rights that interprets moral rights as socially constructed. Hart somehow embraces the dogmatic idea that moral rights, in order to exist, must be pre-given concrete social contexts. I believe that Hart overlooks the possibility of a constructivist theory of moral rights simply because the defense of utilitarianism was too much of a personal project for him. This might also explain why Hart ignores Habermas's version of deontological ethics, a version that does not presuppose the cognitivism of Dworkin's position.

Although I disagree with Hart's argument that utilitarian ethics is the most potent form of critical morality, I welcome the expectation that normative theory should offer a socially relevant critique of conventions. Hart is insistent upon this demand, which he discusses, among other places, in the final lines of "Utilitarianism and natural rights" published in 1978. Concluding his overview of utilitarianism and theories of rights, Hart states:

> The doctrine of human rights has at least temporarily replaced the doctrine of maximizing utilitarianism as the prime philosophical inspiration of political and

> social reform. It remains to be seen whether it will have as much success as utilitarianism once had in changing the practice of governments for human good.[48]

Being a philosophical inspiration for political and social reform is what Hart expects of a plausible normative theory. A closer reading of the essay demonstrates that Hart regards the criterion of political progressivity as bound up with a demand for "clarity and detailed articulation."[49] How, then, is utilitarianism progressive, and how does it avoid the problems that Hart associates with the idea of moral rights?

In his 1973 essay, "The Demystification of the Law," Hart compares his favorite utilitarian philosopher of law, Jeremy Bentham, with Karl Marx. This comparison, I argue, is the key to understanding why Hart dismisses right-based theories and instead endorses utilitarianism. As Hart writes:

> Notwithstanding these great differences[50] of both temperament and political thought, Bentham and Marx agreed on two fundamental points which are relevant to my present theme: first, that their tasks as social thinkers were to clear men's minds as to the true character of human society, and, secondly, that human society and its legal structure which had worked so much human misery, had been protected from criticism by myths, mysteries, and illusions, not all of them intentionally generated, yet all of them profitable to interested parties. [. . .] For both of them such mystery was made possible by the failure on the part of ordinary men to realize that the forms of law and human society were at bottom merely human artefacts, not natural necessities but things actually made by men, and hence things which could be unmade and remade.[51]

Moral or basic rights seem to presuppose the mystification of social conventions, thereby preventing political thought from approaching legal structures and other social institutions critically, as "merely human artifacts."

Hart's skepticism toward a moral realism of natural law that might find its way into the modern theory of rights is reasonable. However, his main argument against right-based political and legal theory as dependent on moral realism of natural law seems to be that the theory of natural law was historically to sustain the mystification of law (and, with it, the political order). Hart identifies a politically progressive element, that is, having transformative potential, in Bentham's definite rejection of the very existence of *natural* law. "Law," he writes, "is something men add to the world, not find within it."[52]

Furthermore, Bentham has revealed the emotive meaning of legal language. There is no pre-given moral order that the law should depict and sustain. Yet, the very idea that there exists such an order, which conservative ideologies merely describe, is a mystification of social relations. Indeed, "to mystify may be to cloak tyranny." "The maintenance of law and order" is in fact the emotive *enforcement* of law.[53] According to Hart, Bentham realizes how "order" (itself a product of power and volition) is de-politicized by conservative ideologies that suppress opposition.

What Bentham, like Marx, saw clearly was that rights and duties are social constructions that can be remade by democratic politics and legislation. Contrary to Marx, Bentham rejected the legitimacy of revolution on the grounds of its anarchical elements. Although Hart seeks to downplay Bentham's anti-revolutionary sentiments, it is clear that Bentham was himself equally devoted to the idea that valid law must not satisfy the criterion of moral duty and that any disobedience to law on moral grounds demands careful deliberation.

We are now in a position to conclude that Hart's defense of utilitarianism and his skepticism toward theories of rights are based on his experience of utilitarianism as a tradition whose historical association with social constructivism makes it a possible critical approach to treating social norms (legal and moral) as conventional, men-made norms. The question that Hart raises, albeit without definitely answering, is whether there is an essential, rather than historically contingent, relationship between politically transformative social constructivism and utilitarian normative theory.

In any case, Hart seems to believe that all theories of basic rights overlook the social character of legitimate moral and legal norms. To Hart, the deontological elements of rights theory cannot but lead to foundationalism. In his later writings, he considers the idea of developing a theory of rights based on a utilitarian justification of right claims. Rejecting such a strategy, Hart states:

> For the content of such utilitarian entitlements would fluctuate with changing circumstances and have none of the stability over time and consequent availability as guides to action both for the right-holder and others which are strongly associated with the notion of rights whenever the notion is employed.[54]

It is obvious that Hart endorses both a utilitarian sensitivity to the importance of context for the justification of norms, and the view that non-legal rights, if meaningfully used, must transcend contextual fluctuation. In practice, Hart's defense of utilitarianism is mostly an endorsement of social constructivism that simultaneously rejects the metaphysics of natural rights. He rejects the possibility of a reasonable theory of rights that does not include "stability over time" as its crucial element.

Hart's political and academic experiences have shown him that theories of moral rights tend to include naturalism and therefore contribute to the "mystification" of legal and political orders that in fact are social products. An example, which confirms Hart's intuition that naturalism in practice mystifies moral and legal conventions, is John Finnis's attack on Hart, his former tutor. After Hart's death, Finnis accused Hart of "the falling away from the level of Plato, Aristotle and Mill to the essentially unphilosophical and irrelevant dialectic with Devlin."[55] Finnis continues by defining the genuinely philosophical question as that of "*elements of individual and social makeup [...] presupposed by political institutions capable* of upholding justice and freedom and the practice of political philosophy itself."[56] In an illustration of Hart's fears about political conservatism with regard to essentialism in rights-based theories, Finnis identifies these "presupposed elements" with a European moral and political culture that he sees as under threat from "reverse colonization."[57] In this case, even a modified form of natural law theory endorses the idealism of a European philosophy that far too often legitimizes imperialism within and between different cultures.

In much the same mode, Dworkin has identified the principles stipulated by the U.S. Constitution as the objective, true principles of justice. It seems to me that Dworkin, even after reading Hart's famous postscript to *The Concept of Law*, failed to realize that Hart recognized the political and legal relevance of critical morality while simultaneously remaining skeptical of any form of moral naturalism.

Hart's own experiences led him to observe, correctly, that deontological theories tend to include either metaphysical or rationalistic foundationalism. However, these instances should not prevent us from further examination of the issue of whether deontological theory is *necessarily* connected to naturalism or quietism. Liam Murphy, in his analysis of Hart's understanding of politics, floats the idea that utilitarianism is not logically connected to "the positivist's political claim [. . .] that an alert and critical attitude toward the legal system is desirable because a legal and political culture where this sceptical attitude prevails is more likely to progress towards substantive justice (away from injustice) [. . .] on the other."[58] As Murphy notes, the social basis of norms and rules was crucial for Hart's theorizing. Murphy further develops Hart's social concept of law by introducing into it more explicated sociological elements, including the legal regime or how people conceive of law differently. However, in his analysis of Hart, Murphy refrains from making a deeper examination of normative ethics, ethical theory, and politics in Hart's thinking. Let us therefore move into this direction.

## IS UTILITARIANISM NATURALLY DEMOCRATIC?

Two elements of Hart's theory are of particular importance for my interpretation and critique of his version of legal positivism. First, Hart endorses moral pluralism by both recognizing it as an essential element of social life and valuing it as an expression of liberal freedom and democracy. As we have seen, moral realism of traditional natural law theory, which, in many cases, also characterizes theories of moral rights, is therefore interrogated by Hart as part of his defense of the sociality (what he calls "man-made character") of moral values. In my interpretation, Hart's critique of natural law and theories of rights is highly productive because it inspires us to take a constructivist approach at the metaethical level. Such a constructivism includes understanding humans as capable agents of social transformation. In turn, this transformation is not directed toward any pre-given and rationally comprehensible aim. Rather, it is an ongoing democratic effort to change society in the direction of greater freedom.

Hart's own engagement in legal discussions in Great Britain attests to this belief. Hart has passionately defended liberal democracy, arguing that the legal enforcement of positive morality should be avoided unless it can be demonstrated that the very preservation of society is in danger. Moreover, this preservation does not have intrinsic value but is rather an instrument for securing existential conditions for individuals.[59]

Hart is consistent in his endorsement of freedom as freedom from coercion and, unlike many contemporary liberal imperialists, accepts pluralism between societies and cultures as reasonable. Most importantly, he recognizes the fact of fundamental inequality on the international level and points out the dominance of strong states as a serious, though not fatal, challenge to legitimacy of the international law. This challenge consists in the limits of legitimate coercion when norms of the international law are enforced.[60]

Second, Hart's view of morality and law incorporates an important materialistic component. As already noted, Hart admits that both conventional norms (positive morality) and the priorities among principles of critical morality are related to the material interests of individuals and social groups. Importantly, Hart recognizes that law secures the social domination and coercion of dominated groups. He admits that human history witnesses

> that, though a society to be viable must offer *some* of its members a system of mutual forbearances, it need not, unfortunately, offer them to all. [. . .] if a system of rules is to be imposed by force on any, there must be a sufficient number who accept it voluntarily. Without their voluntary co-operation, thus creating *authority*, the coercive power of law and government cannot be established. But coercive power [. . .] may be used to subdue and maintain, in a position of permanent inferiority, a subject group whose size, relatively to the master group, may be large or small, depending on the means of coercion, solidarity, and discipline available to the latter, and the helplessness or inability to organize of the former.[61]

Despite this clearly articulated insight into the connection between law and social domination on behalf of power groups in a society, Hart does not regard domination as an essential component of the institution of law. As the quotation above shows, Hart believes that authority is *created* by voluntary cooperation and that it *can be used* in order to dominate.

Moreover, Hart considers the "approximate equality of men"—together with human vulnerability, limited altruism and resources, and limited understanding and strength of will—to be a truism of social life. In Hobbesian style, he writes: "no individual is so much more powerful than others, that he is able, without co-operation, to dominate or subdue them for more than a short period."[62] The comparison between municipal and international law mentioned earlier confirms my interpretation that Hart does not view social inequality within a society as a negation of this "approximate equality." For him, social inequality and domination are contingent rather than constitutive phenomena of social life and law. We need to remember here that Hart is trying to offer a theory about the relationship between law, morality, and coercion. Using "coercion," not power, as a starting point for his analysis, Hart tends to reduce social domination to explicit (albeit not basic) forms of domination such as direct coercion by the state.

Even as he remains critical of social domination, Hart concentrates his critique on a form of coercion that restricts individual freedom within the domain of private, mostly sexual, morality. This reduction becomes both obvious and problematic when Hart discusses the issue of protecting minorities in a democracy. He famously describes the ideal normative position of a democratic politician as acting on "his duty to do what he thinks right, and then to accept his dismissal if he cannot persuade the majority to retain him."[63] This ideal politician is always under a temptation to follow the majority opinion and suppress minorities as a way to stay in power. It is therefore crucial to firmly restrict the legal means of enforcing popular morality. Hitherto Hart's defense of pluralistic democracy is both reasonable and relevant. However, Hart reduces the popular morality that should be kept outside the domain regulated by law (in order to protect individuals and minorities) to mostly issues of personal choices that do not call into question society's fundamental economic and social structures. According to Hart, the markers of the popular attitude of moral conservatism of which a democratic legislator should remain skeptical are "intolerance, indignation, and disgust."[64]

How, then, should Hart's democratic politician deal with popular morality within the domain of social justice beyond traditional liberal freedoms? Are there any tools with a fundamentally structural character in Hart's thinking with which to productively approach the risk of suppressing social groups and individuals? How should a democracy construct its law in order to enable progressive politics in the domain of the distribution of economic, political, and social power?

The relationship between law, politics, and morality in social and economic spheres, although mentioned by Hart, is fundamentally underdeveloped in his theory. In my view, this can be explained by his endorsement of utilitarianism—or, rather, the nature of his endorsement. As already noted, Hart regarded the classical utilitarianism of Bentham and Mill as the historically most progressive political ethics. Yet, he has never subjected it to ideological scrutiny. The most important evidence of this lacuna is the contrast between Hart's critique of theories of natural rights and his defense of utilitarianism. On the one hand, he is critical of deontological ethics of rights for its incapacity to transparently prioritize between rights. On the other, he accepts a utilitarian position that cannot solve the challenge of priorities between legitimate preferences and interests without suppressing socially dominated minorities. Hart believes that minorities are free to argue for their perspectives and to try to convince the majority. His belief in the power of rational argument may be sympathetic but it is obviously naïve to think that freedom of argumentation alone can secure social justice.

As we have seen, Hart is critical of right-based theories because they tend to include metaphysical elements. By presenting conventional norms as corresponding to pre-given natural morality, theories of natural rights legitimize norms that can and should be subjected to moral scrutiny and political change. According to Hart, utilitarianism avoids this risk. Instead of metaphysical foundations, it offers instruments for a democratic critique of human-made law.

Does utilitarianism have any other advantages than this proclaimed "immunity against metaphysics?" If a social group is dominated, socially and economically, and if this domination is reflected in law, how does utilitarianism help the group—other than by rejecting the possibility of legitimizing domination as "natural?"

In my view, Hart delivers a highly valuable critique of natural rights so long as we approach law, morality, and politics from the position of those who possess power or at least have a reasonable chance of getting it. Hart's "democratic politician" should not regard the law of his democracy as an incarnation of natural and universal rights. Nor should the legal or political philosopher. In this perspective, I find Hart's critique of Dworkin plausible. To identify any contextual interpretation of and prioritization between rights as *the* expression of objective values is essentially undemocratic and can easily become anti-liberal. This is especially true when legal or political conventions about rights on behalf of a global superpower, such as the United States, are presented as a universal morality.

However, Hart has no argument against the contention that different versions of legally protected rights can and should be scrutinized by means of a moral vision of universal human rights. For the dominated within a particular social order (including that of democracy), a theory of universal rights offers a powerful inspiration for political resistance to contextual forms of social injustices. Various forms of exploitation, marginalization, racism, and lack of power become visible in light of the idea that everyone should be entitled to equal respect on the basis of their shared humanity. If we use the criterion that Hart introduces when endorsing Bentham's utilitarianism, namely "appeal to practical men,"[65] we can argue that a belief in universal rights can be a rationale for political mobilization to make justified moral claims into positive law.

Most importantly, Hart overlooks the fact that universal rights need not be understood as trans-contextual, objective rights that are uniformly implemented in a political and social culture. There is an egalitarian interpretation of universal rights that avoids this metaphysical trap and simultaneously offers political, moral, and legal resources for social transformation. On such an interpretation, universal rights are legitimate claims, albeit prioritized and implemented contextually, and incompatible with discrimination. This moral political idea has been given a positive legal form in the anti-discrimination clause included in most human rights conventions. As Article 2 of the *International Covenant on Civil and Political Rights* stipulates:

> Each State Party to the present Covenant undertakes to respect and to ensure to all individuals within its territory and subject to its jurisdiction the rights recognized in the present Covenant, without distinction of any kind, such as race, colour, sex, language, religion, political or other opinion, national or social origin, property, birth or other status.

Although there is space for legitimate differences in how states interpret and prioritize rights, the convention stipulates that discrimination is incompatible with the proper protection of human rights. Yet another advantage of human rights morality is its ability to ensure social justice for minorities by constraining the view that democracy is merely an aggregation of social preferences.[66]

My main objection to Hart's utilitarianism is therefore that it overlooks possession or lack of power as a key marker of different social perspectives on law and morality. Hart is right in that various forms of coercion can be legitimized by a belief in the natural character of rights. Rights are always socially constructed. Yet, a belief in moral rights on behalf of those who are not granted legal rights is a powerful tool of social transformation. Such transformation has historically required social revolution. The rights-based critique of inequality recognizes this highlighting importance of social structures rather than freedom of individual choice. Furthermore, the theory of rights can justify radical demands for equal access to power.

Hart's view that individual freedom to argue and to vote is all we need offers a minimalist version of social justice in a democracy. How should we explain Hart's democratic minimalism? In my view, his rejection of radical politics and social revolution is an element of his version of utilitarian political ethics. In fact, Hart has considered the hypothesis that the fear of revolution explains Bentham's opposition to the idea of natural rights. What Hart describes as "the panic-stricken rhetoric" of Bentham's attack on the U.S. Declaration of Independence[67] is of great importance for the skepticism toward moral rights in Bentham's and Mill's utilitarianism that Hart himself has inherited.

The idea of universal rights is radical when used by dominated people demanding freedom and social equality. This is why even today human rights tend to be depoliticized and reduced to positive regulations in municipal legal systems. At the same time, the rhetoric of universal moral rights is invoked when powerful states challenge *other* states' politics or seek to legitimize their involvement in other countries.

In conclusion, the most important and—to use his own terminology—"politically progressive" component of Hart's theory of law and morality is a critique of moral realism incorporated in the natural law theory and a defense of social constructivism. Norms, both legal and moral, are man-made conventions and there is no objective morality to which they must correspond. This constructivism supports the main normative thesis of Hart's positivism, namely that although legal systems include a claim to legitimate authority, there is no moral obligation to obey legal rules solely on the grounds that they are valid laws. Whether such an obligation exists is always a matter of moral judgment.

Furthermore, and most importantly, it is the moral and political judgment of citizens, not the theoretical judgment of legal professionals, that should be used to scrutinize the moral quality of law. Hart is right to argue that natural rights' theories risk legitimizing injustices when they stipulate that law must satisfy fundamental moral criteria in order to be valid law. This is especially true when lawyers are expected to secure that the law satisfies the fundamental moral criteria.[68]

That said, Hart's critique of natural rights is not decisive for those choosing between utilitarianism and right-based normative theory as a way of making a moral and political critique of positive law. While it is crucial to distinguish between law and morality, as well as between conventional and critical morality, such a distinction is never definitely secured by any normative theory. A constructivist theory of moral rights can sustain the separation thesis while utilitarianism can be combined with moral realism. We can invoke Hart's own approach to critical morality in order to illustrate this point.

As already noted, Hart firmly believes that any conventional morality can and should be approached critically. When reflecting on the normative basis of such critique in his lectures on "Law, Liberty, and Morality," Hart formulates two reasonable assumptions. The first is that "the actual institutions of any society, including its positive morality, are open to criticism," and the second is "the critical principle, central to all morality, that human misery and the restriction of freedom are evils."[69] Moreover, occasionally Hart admits that there might exist universal moral values and universal moral virtues. Those values are "individual freedom, safety of life, and protection from deliberately inflicted harm."[70] Universal moral virtues are "self-discipline and control in adapting [the individual's] conduct to a system of reciprocal claims."[71]

How should we evaluate Hart's concessions to universalism, given his famous questioning of the universalism of natural rights theories? Is it the case that Hart envisages universal utilitarian values in place of the principles of natural law that he has rejected? I believe that he does and that the most plausible explanation for this inconsistency is his endorsement, discussed above, of liberal pluralism and liberal democracy on one hand and his recognition of the existence of critical morality on the other. Hart, it would seem, regards individual freedom, safety, and protection from harm as principles of critical morality that are always more open to democratic pluralism than any configuration of "natural rights." At the same time, Hart believes that such utilitarian openness does not lead to political anarchy with regard to the positive legislation that results from political struggle justified by natural rights. In sum, Hart's defense of utilitarianism is, in fact, ideological because it presupposes liberalism as the most progressive ideology of human liberation. Such an assumption is naturally controversial. Moreover, utilitarianism always runs the risk of legitimizing the suppression of minorities as well as perpetuating other political and legal injustices related to democratic populism.

In my view, Hart's philosophy of law offers a good platform for developing a theory of rights that takes seriously the distinction between law and morality while simultaneously avoiding the moral realism of natural rights, which, as Hart has demonstrated, is anti-democratic and anti-liberal. Such a theory must incorporate Hart's insight that the traditions of natural law and natural rights tend to legitimize imperialism at a global level and quietism at the national level. Additionally, any theory of rights must include a constructivist view of social norms by relating them to the material positions of persons and groups. Finally, a plausible theory or rights must offer a vision for democratically mobilizing real people against concrete forms of social injustice.

## NOTES

1. Herbert L.A. Hart, *The Concept of Law*. Third edition (Oxford, UK: Oxford University Press, 2012), 187.

2. Ibid., 17.
3. Ibid., 213.
4. Ibid., 94.
5. Ibid., 98.
6. Ibid., 198.
7. Ibid., 201.
8. Ibid., 203.
9. Ibid., 116.
10. Ibid., 207.
11. Ibid., 172.
12. Ibid., 173–175.
13. Ibid., 229.
14. Ibid., 175–178.
15. Ibid., 178–179.
16. Ibid., 179–180.
17. Ibid., 209.
18. Ibid., 230. See also Chapter IX of *The Concept of Law*.
19. Ibid., 267.
20. Ibid., 250.
21. Herbert L.A. Hart, "Positivism and the Separation of Law and Morals," *Harvard Law Review* 71, no. 4 (1958): 607–610.
22. Ibid., 611.
23. Even in his response to Hart's comments on their disagreements, Dworkin proceeds to call political values for "real" and propositions of law for "true or untrue." This is a sharp contrast to Hart's rejection of value objectivism, to which we will soon return in our analysis. Ronald Dworkin, "Hart's Postscript and the Point of Political Philosophy," in Dworkin, *Justice in Robes* (Cambridge, Massachusetts: Harvard University Press, 2006), 154; 163–164.
24. Hart, *The Concept of Law*, 1.
25. Hart, "Positivism and the Separation of Law and Morals," 595.
26. Ibid., 596.
27. Neil MacCormick gives a nuanced description of this part of Hart's philosophy. Neil MacCormick, *H.L. Hart*. Second Edition (Stanford, CA: Stanford Law Books, 2008), 61–72.
28. Herbert L.A. Hart, *Law, Liberty, and Morality* (Stanford, CA: Stanford University Press, 1963), 20.
29. Hart calls moral realism, that is, the position that there exist objective moral facts, controversial. Hart, *The Concept of Law*, 253.
30. Hart, "Positivism and the Separation of Law and Morals," 597.
31. Herbert L.A. Hart, "Social Solidarity and the Enforcement of Morality," in Hart, *Essays in Jurisprudence and Philosophy* (Oxford, UK: Clarendon Press, 1983), 248. This view of natural law is present already in *The Concept of Law*.
32. Hart, "Positivism and the Separation of Law and Morals," 618.
33. Radbruch's thesis is challenged by historians who have demonstrated how Nazi judges often went beyond what was officially required by the law to anticipate

the underlying will of the *Fuhrer*." Ingo Muller, *Hitler's Justice. The Courts of the Third Reich* (Cambridge, MA: Harvard University Press, 1991), 73.

34. Hart, "Positivism and the Separation of Law and Morals," 617. Hart uses Fuller's translation of Radbruch in this presentation of his position.

35. Hart, "Positivism and the Separation of Law and Morals," 619.

36. Ibid., 620.

37. Hart, *The Concept of Law*, 204.

38. MacCormick, *H. L. Hart*, 97.

39. Herbert L.A. Hart, "Natural Rights: Bentham and John Stuart Mill," in Hart, *Essays on Bentham. Jurisprudence and Political Theory*, 90.

40. Herbert L.A. Hart, "Between Utility and Rights," in Hart, *Essays in Jurisprudence and Philosophy*, 207.

41. Hart did not share Nozick's ideological preferences either.

42. Herbert L.A. Hart, "Between Utility and Rights," in Hart, *Essays in Jurisprudence and Philosophy*, 221.

43. Hart admits the existence of universal values of individual freedom, safety of life, and protection from deliberately inflicted harm. We will discuss this thesis later on.

44. Dworkin, "Hart's Postscript and the Point of Political Philosophy," 164.

45. For obvious reasons, republican theoreticians are more sensitive to the endorsement of pluralism present in Hart. See for example Philip Pettit, "The Basic Liberties," in *The Legacy of H.L.A. Hart: Legal, Political, and Moral Philosophy,* eds. Matthew Kramer, Claire Grant, Ben Colburn, and Antony Hatzistavrou (Oxford, UK: Oxford University Press, 2008), 201–221.

46. Hart, "Between Utility and Rights," 211.

47. Ibid., 213.

48. Herbert L. A. Hart, "Utilitarianism and Natural Rights," in Hart, *Essays in Jurisprudence and Philosophy*, 196–197.

49. Ibid., 195.

50. According to Hart, Bentham is a reformer, while Marx is a utopian thinker. Furthermore, Marx is of the view that social equality is the fundamental value, while in Bentham "equality was always to be subordinate to security." Herbert L.A. Hart, "The Demystification of the Law," in Hart, *Essays on Bentham. Jurisprudence and Political Theory*, 25.

51. Ibid., 25–26.

52. Ibid., 26.

53. Ibid., 27.

54. Hart, "Natural Rights: Bentham and John Stuart Mill," 86.

55. John Finnis, "H.L.A. Hart: A Twentieth-Century Oxford Political Philosopher," *The American Journal of Jurisprudence* 54 (2009): 181.

56. Ibid., 182.

57. Ibid., 180.

58. Liam Murphy, "The Political Question of the Concept of Law," in *Hart's Postscript: Essays on the Postscript to "The Concept of Law,"* ed. Jules L. Coleman (Oxford Scholarship Online, 2001), 399.

59. Hart, *Law, Liberty, and Morality*, 70.
60. Hart, *The Concept of Law*, 195.
61. Ibid., 201.
62. Ibid., 195.
63. Hart, *Law, Liberty, and Morality*, 81.
64. Ibid.
65. Hart, "The Demystification of the Law," 39.
66. Hart admits this function of rights in his *Law, Liberty, and Morality*, 79.
67. Hart, "Natural Rights: Bentham and John Stuart Mill," 80.
68. Hart's position does not imply that lawyers cannot take a stand against immoral law. In my reading, his position is that they can and should do so as citizens.
69. Hart, *Law, Liberty, and Morality*, 82.
70. Ibid., 70.
71. Ibid., 71.

# *Chapter 4*

# Joseph Raz

## *The Legitimate Authority of the Law and Political Morality*

> While there are necessary connections between morality and how the law is, the more significant necessary connections relate to the evaluative perspective which informs our thinking of how the law ought to be.[1]

Joseph Raz has proposed a form of legal positivism that in many regards resembles Hart's positivism. Like Hart, Raz is interested in scrutinizing the law both morally and politically for the sake of political and legal reforms. Raz, whose position on the normativity of law is influenced by the critique of legal positivism developed by natural law theorists, is highly conscious of the different forms that natural law theory can take.[2] Crucially for this study, Raz holds that law is "essentially a form of social organization" rather than "essentially moral."[3] At the same time, he argues that a crucial feature of law as an instrument of social cooperation is its *claim* to the possession of legitimate—that is, moral—authority.

In this chapter, I offer an interpretation of the legal positivism defended by Raz. My purpose is not to give a comprehensive account of Raz's theory, but rather to focus on his understanding of the dialectics of legal and moral normativity. It is essential for the law to present itself as a morally legitimate authority, and this very fact, Raz maintains, makes a moral critique of legal regulations possible and relevant. This understanding, I argue, is reasonable and politically potent. On one hand, a test of legal validity need not include as criteria the moral merits of the law. On the other hand, the claim to legitimate authority on behalf of the law creates a space for a moral critique of legal regulations and for plural political agency.

This chapter develops a critique of Raz that mostly addresses his understanding of how moral evaluation of law should be conducted. An advantage of Raz's theory of law, I show, is its view of law as constitutive of and constituted by political communities.[4] Such communities are the only contexts for a reasonable moral critique of law. What resources are there for such a critique? I agree with Raz's argument that the moral and political critique of law is a contextual enterprise. The critique of law is fundamentally a critique of particular forms of social cooperation. However, such a critique can take several forms; by interpreting it as an "operational moral theory," Raz misses a great deal of the critical potential of political ethics.[5] Although some forms of Kantian ethics and some forms of utilitarianism tend to become an operational theory of this kind, offering direct moral guidance for political action, ethics can and should be conducted as a critical project that aims to reveal concrete forms of social injustice.

Ethics as critique of conventional morality, I argue, can and should assist a democratic critique of law. The category of social justice—tellingly undertheorized by Raz—is a crucial element of such an ethics.

## SOCIAL NORMS AND FUNCTIONS OF THE LAW

Raz considers the law to be a special case of institutionalized normative systems. A normative system of any kind regulates acts permitted by its norms, such as the rules of games. An institutionalized normative system is defined as consisting of "a set of rules some of which institute primary organs and all of which primary organs are bound to act on to the exclusion of all other conflicting reasons."[6] All legal rules are both first-order reasons for acting in a certain way and exclusionary reasons, for instance, reasons for not complying with other reasons. As any other institutional normative system, the law excludes "the application of reasons, standards and norms which do not belong to [it]."[7]

Hence the legal point of view is "an exclusionary point of view": it excludes reasons that, while not legally valid, might nonetheless be valid.[8] In addition, primary organs such as courts are concerned with the authoritative determination of normative situations: their applications of a norm is binding in an authoritative manner, for instance, even if wrong.[9]

Three features of legal systems—comprehensiveness, claim to supremacy, and openness—collectively offer a special case of institutionalized normative systems. Comprehensiveness is the law's claim to regulate any type of behavior, while supremacy is the claim to have the authority "to prohibit, permit or impose conditions on the institutions and operation of all the normative organizations to which members of its subject-community belong."[10] Openness has to do with the ability of legal systems to give binding force to norms that do not belong to them.

This description of the nature of legal systems and the legal point of view is crucial to Raz's understanding of the relationship between law and morality.

Of central importance is the idea that the legal point of view recognizes legal reasons as both first-order reasons and exclusionary reasons, that is, second-order reasons about how to relate to other reasons. This means that some valid moral reasons as well as other valid reasons are excluded by legal reasoning that is correctly conducted—unless they have been posited by the legislator and thus become legally binding.

As I see it, the main argument behind Raz's concept of the law as a special case of institutionalized normative system is the idea that law primarily aims at eliminating practical disagreements between members of a society, including reasonable moral disagreements, in order to secure social cooperation.

In order to further analyze the character of legal normativity, Raz differentiates between justified normativity and social normativity of the law. As it appears in the context of his reading of Hart and Kelsen:

> According to the one view [normativity as justified normativity] legal standards of behavior are norms only if and in so far as they are justified. They may be justified by some objective and universally valid reasons. They may be intuitively perceived as binding or they may be accepted as justified by personal commitment. On the other view [social normativity] standards of behavior can be considered as norms regardless of their merit. They are social norms in so far as they are socially upheld as binding and in so far as the society involved exerts pressure on people to whom the standards apply to conform to them.[11]

Raz argues that a plausible theory of modern law should clearly discriminate between these two forms of normativity, and he regards legal validity as entirely social normativity. He clearly agrees with Hart, who offers "[t]he most successful explanation of the normativity of law in terms of the concept of social normativity."[12] In Hart, legal validity as merely social normativity is finally liberated from the heritage of natural law. While Kelsen still believes that if the law is valid one *ought* to obey it,[13] Raz follows Hart in rejecting this particular element of the natural law tradition.

What, then, is Raz's position on justified normativity apart from his thesis that it should be distinguished from mere social normativity, that is, legal validity? How should we assess the moral quality of valid legal regulations after admitting that it is not an element of legal validity as such?

In approaching this issue, we need to further clarify Raz's position in ethical theory. His critique of Kelsen helps us here. As already noted, Kelsen offers a positivistic theory of law and states that scholars of law should *describe* law, not evaluate it. At the same time, he defends this scientific positivism by presupposing that valid law, from a perspective of the subject of law, implies an obligation to obey such law. Kelsen's idea of the basic norm is a way to explain how legal regulations are regarded as binding by their subjects. While scholars of law should refrain from moral critique of law, the subjects of law presuppose that legal validity has a moral foundation—the basic norm of a particular legal system. In Kelsen, therefore, positivism is a dimension of legal theory rather than a theory of legal normativity as such.

Distancing himself from Kelsen, Raz treats both the theory of law and the theory of morality as domains of practical reason. Legal validity is a variety of social normativity and legal regulations do not imply a moral obligation to obey. However, legal validity is a type of normativity that philosophers of law can and should critically approach. Explaining why and how this can be done, Raz offers a metatheory of justified normativity, that is, an ethical theory.

Raz understands normativity as "features of the world" and he believes that practical rationality is a human capacity to "realize the normative significance of the normative features of the world, and the ability to respond accordingly."[14] To adopt Raz's own terminology, these features of the world are *facts* that constitute reasons to react.[15] As he explains elsewhere: "A [normative] reason for an action is a consideration that renders its choice intelligible, and counts in its favour."[16] Clearly, "facts" in this context are social facts, not nature-like elements of being. Most importantly, Raz uses the phrase "justification of principles" rather than referring to moral beliefs that can be verified or falsified. This allows us to interpret his metaethical position as non-cognitivism. However, Raz does not reduce moral judgments to emotions which makes his position similar to prescriptivism rather than emotivism.

Moral reasons are neither descriptive statements nor entirely emotional attitudes. According to the prescriptivist analysis of morality, practical reasons are reasons for human action. This is often overlooked even by generous interpreters of Raz's positivism. One example is Shivprasad Swaminathan, who has rightly observed some inconsistences in the metaethics of Raz and other legal positivists who endorse non-cognitivism. However, in his critique Swaminathan reduces all forms of non-cognitivism to emotivism and expressivism.[17] According to emotivism, moral judgments express emotions and therefore cannot be scrutinized by reason. On this view, non-cognitivism does not allow for rational scrutiny of moral quality of posited norms. Prescriptivism, by contrast, regards moral judgments as prescriptions or imperatives for human action, thereby avoiding reducing moral judgment to its emotional component. What Swaminathan misses, then, is that prescriptivism, unlike emotivism, allows for a combination of metaethical non-cognitivism and rationalism within metaethics as well as normative ethics. The interpretation of moral judgments as practical prescriptions is combined with an endorsement of the rational and intersubjective scrutiny of practical reasoning.

How then can we do such a scrutiny? Raz does not follow Richard Hare, who famously argued for a prescriptivism combined with the abstract principle of universalizability as the fundamental form of rational moral reasoning. Instead, Raz thinks that practical reason is always historical and contextual. He claims that "the substantive principles of [practical] reason are historical products which can be challenged on grounds of self-contradiction, incoherence, and unreliability, and which can change to avoid such challenges."[18] Elements of rational scrutiny are present in practices that are basically contingent and contextual. This is so because the human ability to reason is central to rationality in any form—"regarding reasons to belief, action, emotion, or anything else."[19]

Practical attitudes such as moral respect for the law accordingly involve a recognition of the moral reasons for obeying the law.[20] In a famous essay titled "Respect for Law," Raz explains how he understands the practical attitude of respect for law. Such an attitude means that its holder has expressive reasons for respecting the law, such as identification with society. Yet, that person can express their loyalty to society by critiquing laws they regard as unjust. Perspectives like these should not be excluded from the analysis of law.

For Raz, moral and legal normativity is both rational and social. Social normativity of the law is clearly related to its social functions, which should be analyzed in such a way as to serve the purposes of reformers.[21] Reformers are interested in the question of what good law in their society should be, not simply in what constitutes valid law of that society. This means that the analytic tools of a plausible theory of law must allow for a critique of law in order to improve its social functionality.

Raz discriminates between direct and indirect functions of the law. The former is fulfilled by the law being obeyed and applied, while the latter relates to the social consequences of knowledge of the existence of law. One such indirect function is the correlation between the introduction of new legal norms and the changing moral conventions of a particular society. Direct functions of the law are either primary or secondary. Regulations of changes and enforcement of the law are secondary functions of the law. There are four primary functions: first, preventing and encouraging behavior; second, providing facilities for private arrangements: third, providing services and redistributing goods; and finally, settling unregulated disputes.[22] This taxonomy, together with the distinction between two normative types of legal rules as either duty imposing or power conferring, offers instruments for the analysis of different particular laws as fundamental regulators of social cooperation.

On a more general level, writes Raz,

> the law is setting up and maintaining schemes of social co-operation, and this not only by providing sanctions to motivate those who would not otherwise contribute their shares [. . .] but also through designating in an open and public

> way what the scheme is and what each has to do as his contribution to it [. . .], thus enabling those who are motivated by the appropriate reasons to take part in the co-operative enterprise.[23]

Above all, the law is an instrument of social cooperation, an instrument that is both constitutive of and constituted by a particular political community.[24] In order for a society to function many disagreements must be eliminated in an authoritative manner; this is precisely what the law does.

However, particular schemes of social cooperation as stipulated by law can and must be evaluated morally. Raz argues that this social cooperation, rather than the law as its instrument, is the genuine feature of the world (facts) to which moral normativity, that is, justified normativity, is a reaction. The law is good if it "reinforces protection of morally valuable possibilities and interests and encourages and supports worthwhile forms of social cooperation."[25]

Social normativity of legal rules may or may not be compatible with moral normativity. This has to do with the fact that the law as an institutionalized normative system provides *authoritative* ways of settling social disputes. As such, it excludes many valid reasons, including moral reasons. If a law is morally justified, it can be justified in different ways. As Raz argues in passage from *Engaging Reason* quoted above, justification can be achieved by means of valid reasons, intuition, or personal commitment. How, then, should a positivistic theory of law that serves reformers understand and evaluate these and related types of justified normativity?

## MORALITY AND LAW: FROM AUTHORITY TO JUSTIFICATION

In his 2003 essay "About Morality and the Nature of Law," Raz formulates his main thesis about the relationship between law and morality by stating that the most significant necessary connection between law and morality "relate[s] to the evaluative perspective which informs our thinking of how law ought to be, rather than how it is."[26] This is so because it is necessary for a binding authority such as the law to claim that it is a morally legitimate authority.

The law always asserts its own legitimacy, presenting itself as a morally justified authority. When describing the character of his own legal positivism, Raz maintains that this positivism "ascribe[s] to the law as an essential feature that it claims legitimate authority, and the concept of legitimate authority is a moral one."[27] The issue of whether a posited law is justified is a moral issue and not an issue of the law's own legal validity. However, it is crucial that Raz regards the claim to legitimate authority as a constitutive feature of the law. He does not believe in the possibility of law that does not present itself as morally justified authority. Whether law is justified is another question, and this dialectics of law—necessarily claiming morally justified authority while in many cases lacking it—makes possible a moral critique of law and, with it, reform.

What, then, is morally justified authority? Raz calls his understanding of such an authority the service conception of legitimate authority. He offers a short summary of this conception in his 2009 essay "The Problem of Authority: Revisiting the Service Conception" in which he endorses the view that authority is a right to rule which "removes the decision from one person to another."[28] In laying claim to its own authority, the law thus demands that its subjects act in accordance with legal rules instead of following other reasons for actions. (We have already learned that all legal rules are exclusionary reasons for acting in a particular way.) This claim in itself cannot constitute a moral obligation to obey the law because such an obligation always presupposes moral justification. Therefore, the moral question which the service conception is an answer to can be formulated as "how can it ever be that one has a duty to subject one's will and judgment to those of another?"[29]

The service conception states that two conditions must be met by an authority's directive in order to be legitimate, for instance, morally binding for its subjects. The first condition is called the normal justification thesis or condition and the second the independence condition:

> First, that the subject would better conform to reasons that apply to him anyway (that is, to reasons other than the directives of the authority) if he intends to be guided by the authority's directives than if he does not [. . .]. Second, that the matters regarding which the first condition is met are such that with respect to them it is better to conform to reason than to decide for oneself, unaided by authority.[30]

Developing the service conception, Raz seeks to reconcile the social need for authority (of law) with the moral ideal of autonomy on behalf of individuals. Social authority can but need not always counteract moral autonomy if autonomy is understood as derived from reasons and personal judgment. This introduces two fundamental restrictions on legitimate authority (here, the authority of law). The first states that obedience to authoritative reasons should not require us to contradict reasons that apply to us anyway. Although I am not expected to carry out a moral inquiry, whenever I obey a legal ruler, these rules—or, rather, the reasons behind them—should not contradict the moral reasoning of such an inquiry. If they do, the law will counteract the individual's ability to moral judgment. The second restriction recognizes the value of direct moral judgment and accordingly requires legitimate law to ensure that the scope of its authority remains proportional.

Authority of the law as an instrument of social cooperation is thus morally legitimate when it promotes human rationality. If the law suppresses the moral autonomy of its subjects, its social authority is morally unjustified. In practice, legitimacy is enjoyed when the rationale for a law can withstand the scrutiny of independent moral reasoning. In Raz's own words, "authority helps our rational capacity whose function is to secure conformity with reason."[31] This normative criterion, what we might call the principle of justification, is a crucial part of Raz's interpretation of political morality—to which we now turn.

## RAZ ON POLITICAL MORALITY

Raz's analysis of legal normativity is plausible in several regards. It considers the law an instrument for social cooperation which, for precisely that reason, claims legitimate authority in order to enjoy de facto social authority. This dialectic makes possible a critique of law, which, in turn, contributes to democratic reform. It is also reasonable to believe that the concrete circumstances of social cooperation, rather than their use of law as an instrument, should be regarded as the primary object of moral scrutiny. What, then, is moral scrutiny of the law, and how should legal regulations be justified?

In an essay from 2004, Raz claims that any principle that can legitimize positive law as well as government is a moral principle. Which principles are moral is defined by their content: "[moral principles] are principles that allow, perhaps even require, some people to interfere in important ways in the lives of others. Valid principles that have such content are moral principles, or nothing is."[32] Raz here reminds us that the normativity of the law is not essentially different from that of morality; both are social regulations. What makes law different from morality is that the former includes some moral considerations and excludes others and does so in an authoritative manner.

As we have seen, Raz believes that particular forms of social cooperation, rather than the law, should be the proper object of critical evaluation. When presenting his own view of political morality, Raz focuses on those public institutions of government that lay claim to the authority "to regulate all aspects of life."[33] Other political agents do not claim such an authority, which Raz views as a sufficient reason to exclude other agents from his analysis of political morality. We will return to this critical assumption but let us first reconstruct the basic elements of Raz's theory of political morality.

This theory is articulated and argued for in *The Morality of Freedom*, in which Raz contends that it should provide "the principles on the basis of which the theory of institutions constructs arguments for having political institutions of this character rather than that."[34] Crucially, however, a theory of political morality is not understood as a critical enterprise, that is, what I am calling a normative theory of political ethics. Instead, Raz regards political morality as moral doctrines similar to *a moral world* of ideologies such as particular types of liberalism or egalitarian doctrines. This much is already clear from his chapter on "Right-Based Moralities," which is instrumental in relation to the main aim of Raz's monograph: to argue in favor of a non-individualistic understanding of freedom as the main principle of political morality. In developing his argument against rights-based theories of political morality, Raz does not discriminate between a normative theory of rights and an analysis of moral conventions and practices of rights. As he writes in *The Morality of Freedom*:

> This chapter argues that neither morality nor political morality is right-based: that if morality has a foundation it includes duties, goals, virtues, etc. [. . .] We are to envisage a moral theory the fundamental principles of which state that certain individuals have certain rights. [. . .] does a correct or sound morality have this structure?[35]

Clearly, Raz does not view a theory of morality (ethics) as a normative theory whose main purpose is to offer tools for a critique of moral conventions. Rather, he sees a theory of political morality as a model of "sound morality," something that can be expected to offer a reasonable understanding of fundamental values such as freedom.

When Raz criticizes different moral theories, he mostly does so by analyzing the values present in those theories. For example, a moral theory can be individualistic "if it is a humanistic morality which does not recognize any intrinsic value in any collective good."[36] In this quotation, it becomes clear that Raz views a moral theory as a kind of ideology,[37] something that is confirmed when he presents the liberal individualism of Ronald Dworkin as *the* model for right-based morality (and later even as the model for egalitarianism). Consequently, Raz calls his own understanding of political freedom "a *doctrine* of political freedom."[38]

Let us recapitulate the main substance of Raz's vision of sound political morality. For Raz, personal autonomy is the most fundamental element of the good life. Understood thus, the good life is that of someone who successfully co-creates it by means of reason-guided actions. In order to exercise autonomy, all individuals need appropriate mental abilities, an adequate range of options (to modify and reasonably choose between), and independence (which means freedom from coercion and manipulation).[39]

Personal autonomy as the crucial element of the good life is the ultimate value that justifies the principle of autonomy which "requir[es] people to secure the conditions of autonomy for all people."[40] This principle is not a value-neutral principle of social cooperation but a perfectionist one: it stipulates that the government has a moral duty to secure morally valuable opportunities for different personal projects. The main justification for Raz's perfectionistic liberalism is his critique of an individualism which assumes that individuals are free to create their life. According to Raz, people do not create their lives; rather, they co-create lives by freely choosing between already existing social forms and by modifying social forms that exist in their communities. Social forms as valuable opportunities for a good life can differ greatly and are not reducible to particular and superior social forms. Sufficiently different cultures can offer a range of such valuable opportunities.

The principle of autonomy offers a criterion for justified limitations to an individual's autonomy. Such limitations are introduced for the sake of the greater autonomy of the others or for the future autonomy of the individual whose autonomy is being temporary restricted (for example, by imprisonment). The principle of autonomy implies that positive freedom is a crucial dimension of political freedom: "the state has the duty not merely to prevent denial of freedom, but also to promote it by creating the conditions of autonomy."[41] Raz himself has noted that his view differs from more common liberal beliefs in that it allows paternalism as a means of creating valuable options for personal choice. Unlike collectivistic doctrines, Raz does not argue in favor of strong centralist government nor does he promote "a radical programme of change through political action."[42]

It seems to me that Raz has, in fact, incorporated elements of the Aristotelian understanding of morality into his view of personal autonomy. It is not essentialist in the same way as Aristoteles's ethics because it rejects the existence of one superior way of realizing human nature (for Aristotle, by virtue of a capacity for speculative reasoning). However, Raz's morality of freedom includes an element of essentialism: the good life is trans-contextually defined as the life of persons successfully developing and accomplishing their own rational projects. Individuals are the subjects of such morally valuable projects, something that explains Raz's frequent use of the terminology of virtues.

Furthermore, Raz views personal well-being—understood as successful completion of individual projects—as the main purpose of legitimate social cooperation. This cooperation is expected to be secured by a government that, like a good parent, takes responsibility for creating morally valuable opportunities for its subjects' personal choices.

The Aristotelian character of Raz's moral doctrine is combined with a communitarian approach to personal morality. The valuable social forms through which individuals should create their lives are contingent and contextual: "Since values are grounded in concrete social forms there is no room for radical political action to secure a fundamental change of social condition. Politics is the art of gradual amelioration."[43] Like other Aristotelian thinkers, Raz invites individuals to exercise their autonomy within the framework of existing social forms. It is, of course, not impossible to imagine that a good life can be framed as a political project. Yet, such a project remains a personal choice that is dependent upon individual autonomy within a preexisting social context.

Hence, Raz does not believe in the possibility of a radical change by means of political action. Nor does he believe in the existence of moral conventions whose deficiency would necessitate a call for radical social transformation. In an essay from 1994 entitled "Moral Change and Social Relativism," Raz argues that morality, unlike law, cannot be totally defective, that is, demanding a complete remake, because its role is to make intelligible various aspects of human life and thus provide guidance.[44]

I think that precisely this understanding of morality as a contextual provision of social guidance for personal life projects explains why Raz adopts a form of teleology in order to discuss social morality as a matter of state responsibility. Raz rarely mentions the category of social justice because he believes that social morality is about the state's responsibility to secure a range of social forms among which individuals can autonomously choose in order to co-create their personal good life.

In practice, Raz defends a communitarian approach to political morality, which raises a challenge always present in communitarian ethics: how does one critically evaluate a moral culture? Communitarian ethics can explain the dynamics of different moral traditions but has little to offer to anyone looking for instruments with which to scrutinize fundamentally unjust social conventions. What does Raz have to say about the existence of unjust forms of social cooperation?

We have learned that different political cultures are justified by means of the principle of autonomy, which must imply that there are cultures that lack legitimacy. This possibility is explicitly mentioned, though not elaborated on, in Raz's discussion of constitutional rights in *The Morality of Freedom*. The constitution, he writes, "affects the existence of the basic political culture, which is—if a good at all—a collective good."[45] A footnote comments that "[N]othing is here implied as to the proper response to a mildly or grossly unjust constitution."[46] The category of injustice appears rather unexpectedly and disappears almost immediately, leaving the reader uncertain about the meaning of injustice in this particular context as well as its implications for Raz's theory of political morality. If nothing here is of significance for how we should respond to unjust political cultures, what is the purpose of political morality?

As I see it, Raz is in fact defending two interrelated ideas, one developed explicitly and one under-theorized. The first, which has already been presented, is that political cultures should be scrutinized against the principle of autonomy. This principle is modified in Raz's thinking, where it acquires a communitarian frame: moral autonomy is not a Kantian ideal of self-legislation but a vision of rational personal choices on the basis of contextually available conventions. If a government offers social forms that make it possible for everyone to autonomously co-create a good life then its authority is justified.

The second idea is that the political cultures that are the objects of Raz's theorizing are basically *just* (or "not unjust" in his terminology) political cultures. Such a reduction of the scope of a theory of law and morality is not plausible, as becomes clear when we learn that in Raz's view most modern societies are not unjust. They could and should be improved and reformed but they need not be radically challenged. Raz's skepticism about the very possibility of radical social change, together with his view that the existence of personal choices of meaningful social forms is the most important social good, account for his evaluation of most non-authoritarian political cultures as basically just. Distributive justice and justice as the critique of other forms of social inequality are not relevant for Raz's analysis of the moral quality of law. In my view, such a reduction of social injustice to direct authoritarian ways of preventing people to realize personally meaningful life projects is deeply problematic.

Before developing this critique of Raz's theory of political morality further, I want to emphasize another important element of this theory, namely his interpretation of political ethics as operational theory. In his 1996 essay "On the Nature of law," Raz argues that both Kantianism and utilitarianism are hoping for operational theories of political morality.[47] Unfortunately, Raz does not elaborate on this point but merely states that he shares the critical position of Bernard Williams. In my view, Raz's main point is that social cooperation is fundamentally contextual, for which reason we should not expect universalistic moral philosophy (what, following Williams, he also calls political moralism) to offer a direct guidance for political action.

Raz believes that Kant, utilitarians, and Rawls[48] are seeking just such an operational theory: they want to offer direct moral guidance to political agents in a democracy. At the same time, they hold that a plausible theory of political morality should offer trans-contextual principles that can be used for evaluating different social institutions. Raz, it would seem, believes that, in contrast to the normative ethics of both Kant and utilitarianism, moral-political doctrines such as his variant of perfectionistic liberalism can offer guidance for social institutions *within* their own contextual spaces.

I have two main objections to this particular interpretation of Western moral philosophy as a kind of a-contextual moralism. In the first place, although some forms of utilitarianism and Kantianism try to offer operational models for guidance of political decisions, others do not. Raz is right in saying that morality as a dimension of social cooperation is fundamentally contextual: it comprises dilemmas and does not allow the existence of universally valid operational models. We can agree that there are several forms of contemporary Kantianism and utilitarianism that tend to create such models.[49] However, it is also obvious that there are versions of moral philosophy, primarily with a Kantian character, to which this objection does not apply. Rather than constructing operational models, such a philosophy focuses on critique of particular social conventions and institutional injustices, as it becomes explicit in the critical versions of Kantian ethics considered later in this study. For critical perspectives of this kind, the "operationality" of political ethics is a theoretical weakness rather than an advantage.

My second objection concerns the fact that Raz disregards the possibility of a normative ethical model that aims to make a critique of social institutions, including the law, and that combines normative universalism with a sensitivity to the contextual and the contingent nature of social institutions. We have already noted that in his essay "On Rationality and Justification of Reason" in *Engaging Reason* Raz explains his own position as a conviction that "[t]he substantive principles of reason are historical products which can be challenged on grounds of self-contradiction, incoherence, and unreliability, and which can change to avoid such challenges."[50] This can be described as a rationalistic communitarianism that allows for a moderate critique of conventional political moralities. However, I will argue that context dependency and the contingency of social morality are compatible with the possibility of a radical moral-philosophical critique. The theory of morality we seek does not allow for the existence of a universal operational morality. Simultaneously it defends a critical form of the principle of universalizability. This makes it possible to ask moral questions about the basic social arrangements in different types of societies.

Before elaborating further on this thesis, I want to present a critique of Raz's understanding of the relationship between law, politics, and morality.

## WHICH LAW? WHOSE POLITICAL MORALITY?

It is an advantage of Raz's position that he consequently considers the law to be an instrument of social cooperation. As with morality, albeit in a different (authoritative) manner, law is a dimension of social life. In order to function properly, for instance, to make social cooperation efficient, the law presents itself as a legitimate authority, thereby creating a possibility of moral critique. Legally valid norms may or may not be justified, but because the law presents its authoritative status as justified, a moral critique of law becomes possible.

"Possible" need not mean that a critique of law is practically possible at all times and in every society; such a possibility is conditioned by several political factors. However, the law's claim to legitimate authority is a fundamental precondition of critique and reforms. Raz himself seems to believe that it is rational for a citizen in a non-authoritarian society to presume that the claim to legitimacy on behalf of law is justified. However, this presumption does not create a moral obligation to obey the law: the latter is always related to the result of moral justification.

Moral justification and the critique of law are a contextual enterprise that neither demands nor presupposes the existence of natural morality. I see in Raz's position here another important advantage of his theory of law and morality. The law is a product of social cooperation as well as the most important instrument of such cooperation; it must be understood and evaluated contextually. Contrary to natural law theory, legal positivism does not presuppose the existence of a universal human morality. Like natural law theory, it allows for a politically relevant moral critique of correctly posited law. But this critique must be developed as a critique of particular types of social cooperation rather than advocacy of a universally valid model for a good society.

Raz is therefore right in combining valuable insights from legal positivism with an endorsement of the possibility of moral critique of law as a means of social reform. Yet, he does not make full use of the critical potential of legal positivism, tending instead to endorse the conventional political morality in place (here, the liberal one). Despite his thesis that the law's claim to legitimate authority makes possible a moral critique of law, Raz does not develop such a critique. Moreover, he argues that it is reasonable for citizens in non-authoritarian societies to view the law as legitimate.

Why does quietism reappear in a theory that begins with the aspiration of empowering reformers? One possible, albeit less thought provoking, explanation of this tendency would be that Raz's communitarianism is liberal in nature and differs only slightly from the dominant political ideology of his own society. As with his attempt to combine some elements of natural law with legal positivism, Raz offers a combination of liberalism and communitarianism. We have already seen how he modifies the meaning of political freedom in order to jettison the unreasonable individualism of many liberal doctrines. Freedom as Raz advocates it is the positive freedom of an individual to autonomously co-create a meaningful life project from preexisting social forms. Liberal culture is thus a culture that offers a range of such meaningful social forms.

In a descriptive perspective, it is plausible to view liberalism as *a culture* waiting to be further developed and moderately reformed: liberal political traditions are traditions and every attempt to deny this risks to elevate particular political settings to the level of universal values such as Democracy or Freedom.[51] On a normative level, however, Raz's particular endorsement of liberalism is connected to the thesis that radical social changes are not possible. His writings give no indication of how radical a change has to be in order to be count as radical. It seems to me that in practice what Raz is denying is the possibility of revolution as an expression of the demand for social equality. I will return to this issue in order to argue for the importance of revolution as a political category for critical analysis of political morality and law. For now, I want to highlight that when Raz rejects the possibility of radical political change, he also abandons the theorizing of social justice.

If most non-authoritarian societies in general and liberal societies in particular are basically just political traditions—what then is injustice? Inequality as defined by different theories of distributive justice, as well as inequality in regard to power, is irrelevant for Raz's analysis of moral quality of the law. In my view, this explains why Raz's theory attaches no practical importance to the voices of those who regard the political tradition of their society as deeply unjust, i.e., those who, according to both Hart and Raz, are forced to obey the law because they have few or none incentives for loyalty to a particular form of social cooperation.

One obvious problem with this position is that it contradicts Raz's own thesis about the nature and function of the law. If the law is to be understood as an instrument of efficient social cooperation, a theory of law should not disregard the radical critique of particular forms of social cooperation on behalf of the disadvantaged. Rather, it should be expected to explicitly take a stand on the role such a critique might have in the dialectic of law, politics, and morality. Otherwise, the theory risks misrepresenting the coercion of social groups as an authentic form of social cooperation.

The exclusion of radical critique of different forms of social cooperation, and thus of the law as its instrument, relates to another feature of Raz's liberal communitarianism. This communitarianism accordingly reduces political morality to an issue of the relationship between a government and its individual subjects. It would be unfair to demand that Raz's theorizing of law and morality include a fully elaborated political theory. However, it is equally problematic to build a general theory of law and morality on the assumption that politics, political morality, and law all center on a relationship between a government and its individual subjects. Political reforms, even less radical ones, are in most cases demanded and promoted by collective agency. This agency can be framed in different ways in different types of democratic and non-democratic societies, but it cannot be explained as a simple aggregation of individual positions vis-à-vis a government.

Raz could respond to this critique by emphasizing that the main point of his theory is precisely the claim that humans, in order to realize their humanity, need a range of meaningful *personal options*, not social justice with its core demand for equality. But if this is so, there can be no connection between legitimate law and democratic inclusion. People with less power or without any access to power can have meaningful personal choices as pure consumers of the state's policies. This view indeed seems to be part of Raz's understanding of social cooperation. Unlike Hart, Raz does not regard democratic inclusion as the most important criterion of progressive politics. People are mostly consumers of what the state has to offer. Even when Raz takes up collective rights, he focuses on the importance of personal membership of a group rather than the demand for political agency on behalf of minorities.

Let us recall the discussion of collective rights in *The Morality of Freedom*. In the first place, Raz states that individual rights such as for example freedom of speech protect a democratic character of the society as a collective good.[52] Then he proceeds by describing the prohibition of discrimination of minorities as a right that secures "their ability to feel pride in membership in groups."[53] Identity, or even just taking pride in a particular identity, is here considered as justification for the prohibition of discrimination against minorities.

My main objection to how Raz justifies collective rights has to do with the fact that identity, belonging, and pride can be achieved in a society in which minorities have radically different access to power and in which the law is deeply unjust. Moreover, the law can transform a lack of power into a minority status in need of hierarchical protection, which is, for example, how legal regulations in patriarchies deal with women. In a range of political settings, including the liberal, women's rights are legally protected to an extent that would satisfy Raz's criterion of prohibition of discrimination even as they maintain the unequal and gendered access to power, that is, patriarchy.

I am therefore critical of Raz when he affirms political morality to be a domain of the relationship between a government and its individual subjects. Even moderate social transformations demand political agency on behalf of different social groups and such transformations typically involve a variety of understandings of structural justice and injustice. This kind of agency cannot be fully secured through political discussions about the range of valuable social forms for personal projects. Social justice, or, rather, the lack thereof, becomes an issue—descriptively as well as normatively—whenever disadvantaged groups enter political space. This insight must be incorporated into any theory that aspires to formulate criteria for legitimate legal authority.

Above all, I also believe that Raz's understanding of political morality as doctrine prevents him from formulating the critique of law that is allowed for by his own notion of law's claim to legitimacy. Instead of using ethics to scrutinize law as the instrument for concrete forms of social cooperation, he uses a revised version of liberalism as the legitimization of the authority of the law. In practice, the result is a legitimization of the state as *the* subject of politics and law.

This becomes obvious when Raz explains his understanding of human rights. Let us recall Raz's position. In positivistic style,[54] he starts with the claim that a reasonable theory of human rights must follow "the dominant trend in human rights practice," for instance, "a right is a human right as a defensibly sufficient ground for taking action against violators in the international arena."[55] He believes that his understanding of human rights as the ground for legitimate international actions represents a development of the political conception of human rights. Such a conception differs from "traditional philosophical attempts" to explain human rights as rights that are related in various ways to the naturalistically interpreted humanity of all people. In contrast to these traditional approaches, a political approach considers human rights as fundamental for social cooperation (Rawls) and concrete social practices (Raz). According to Raz, human rights are "the moral limits of state sovereignty [. . .] determined not merely by the moral limits to the authority of states but also by the possibility of morally sound interference by others."[56]

I can think of several interpretations of what this conception of human rights actually means. Concrete practices of human rights do not lie beyond reasonable critique. Raz knows this and acknowledges the existence of colonial structures in the global world, which allows us to assume that his agenda is to reduce the range of possible international sanctions, which are legitimized by the rhetoric of human rights.[57] Another possibility would be simply to interpret Raz's concept of human rights as a description of the most dominant discourse within the international human rights law rather than practice of international law. In any case, what is critical is the fact that Raz does not view human rights as an instrument of political struggle about the meaning of social justice within nation states. He differs from both Rawls and Hart in this regard. As we have seen, Hart views human rights as either political achievements by those who experience injustices, or rhetorical nonsense. Raz considers human rights to be identical with human rights as understood and to some extend practiced within the domain of international law.[58]

As applied to human rights or discussions of legitimate legal authority in a state, Raz's theory of law and morality would benefit from a more critical understanding of political ethics. Such, at least, is my own view. He starts by arguing for the importance of the moral critique of law but ends by reducing this critique to the issue of legitimate state power exercised over individuals. The social justice perspective is lacking in his theory of law and morality, something that in turn impacts Raz's view of democratic politics.

In the previous chapter, I criticized Hart's view of morality for reducing the moral critique of law to an individual dimension of injustice. However, one great advantage of his position is the clearly articulated democratic ethos that Hart finds in the classical utilitarian critique of law. For Hart, a critique of social regulations must be based on the actual positions and preferences of citizens in a democracy. However, in trying to overcome the individualism of Hart's version of liberalism, Raz sets democracy apart from the institutions and practices of social critique. Seeking a less individualistic theory that would contribute to reforms of law, he creates a theory that reduces such a critique to a theory of the relationship between the state and individuals as consumers of legal regulations and politics of the state.

Hart is clear about the need for ethics as a critique of conventions and he believes that utilitarianism offers the best model for a critical morality with progressive political potential. Raz does not see this need but instead views political morality as mostly an analysis of doctrines, traditions, and ideologies. For him, liberalism is a particular political tradition that can be developed and improved but not radically questioned. Although Raz is right on a descriptive level in regarding different political ideologies as traditions, such a view gives up the demand for social justice. Unjust traditions, or the unjust elements of traditions, must be exposed by critical ethics in ways that go beyond making moderate reforms to existing traditions.

Where does this leave us? Raz develops a legal positivism that, like Hart's, allows for a moral critique of law. Moreover, this positivism is framed as a justification of the importance of such a critique. The critical element of this justification is the firm distinction between the issue of legal validity and that of moral quality of the law. While legal validity does not include moral criteria, the law necessarily claims its own moral legitimacy. This claim is a social phenomenon, that is, a feature of law as a social institution, rather than a normative dimension of the concept of law. For this very reason, the moral critique of law is a socially relevant enterprise. Because the law, being an instrument of social cooperation, *claims* that its authority is morally legitimate, a moral critique of law is relevant for its social legitimacy. The service conception of legitimate authority includes criteria for questioning the social claim on behalf of legal systems. To demonstrate that a legal system demanding obedience violates morally valid reasons, or that the scope of this expectation is too broad, represents a serious challenge to this system's legitimacy.

How, then, should a moral critique of law be framed? Unlike most natural law theorists, Hart and Raz do not believe in the existence of a universal human nature that justifies the moral validity of norms and rules. Rather, they look for instruments for a moral critique of the law in the domain of political morality by focusing on concrete forms of social cooperation. Raz tries to overcome the individualism of many other forms of liberalism (Hart's included) by combining the liberal endorsement of personal freedom with a communitarian understanding of freedom as the co-creation of one's life from a range of pre-given alternatives. Although this combination allows for the recognition of the plurality of legitimate political cultures, it entirely overlooks the issue of social justice. The law of a political culture that incorporates severe forms of inequality is effectively presented as legitimate because the government is securing meaningful choices on a personal level.

In "Disagreement in Politics," an article published in 1998, Raz describes his position on political morality and democratic politics as a kind of historical pragmatism. He writes: "I am inclined toward a position which is informed by moral concerns but regards their application as a thoroughly nuanced and pragmatic matter."[59] Critiquing different forms of political moralism—from Rawls to Waldron—Raz argues that historical contingency is in practice far more important as a dimension of legitimate political arrangements than moral principles open to rational deliberation. Societies that prove the historical stability of their constitutional arrangements are viewed by Raz as the most important context for the discussion of legitimate principles of political morality.[60] Although Raz's critique of political moralism is very useful, his own position on constitutional disagreements is a defense of social stability (against radicalism inspired by moral visions of justice) rather than of democracy.

My view is that Raz, as a result of his position on critical morality, ultimately formulates a variety of legal positivism that does not challenge any political culture except the obviously totalitarian. Another problem is that he ignores several important social subjects and political agents, choosing instead to focus entirely on individuals and governments. While personal freedom as Raz understands it is a reasonable criterion of political morality, many forms of injustice are neither constructed nor effectively resisted in terms of a personal freedom to make meaningful choices.

Most structural injustices do not involve the relationship between government and individual subjects, a fact that political ethics must recognize. Contemporary forms of racism and sexism are only two examples of such structural injustice. In most European countries, there is legislation in place to protect women's rights and combat racism. This legislation, which is progressive in comparison with earlier forms of patriarchy and racism in Europe, coexists relatively peacefully with normalized inequalities with regard to both economic, social, and discursive power. Whenever underprivileged groups demand more power instead of individual protection, the representatives of privileged groups argue forcefully against the legitimacy of their demands. Raz's Aristotelian ethics, though combined with a highly reasonable form of legal positivism, fails to expose this dynamic as an object for critique.

Furthermore, neither individuals nor governments reasonably can be expected to be a driving force behind radical social transformation. Social injustices affect individuals but are structured or destroyed through collective agency. Addressing injustices therefore requires admitting the existence of collective political agency beyond the relationship between individuals and government. Bearing in mind Raz's own firm rejection of totalitarianism, it is important to highlight that a reduction of the society to individuals directly subjected to the government is one of the most efficient mechanism of keeping totalitarian societies intact.[61]

If I am right, Raz weakens the critical potential of legal positivism by overlooking the importance of collective social subjectivity and social justice. Instead of being a theory that serves the reformer, his positivism becomes a legitimization of any law that happens to be in place unless it is obviously totalitarian. Non-totalitarian societies, liberal societies included, are often marked by profound democratic deficit. This deficit appears in many forms and demands a sharp critique of legal arrangements *as unjust*. Such a critique of law should not be reduced to a critique of the exercise of power on behalf of the state.

Finally, I agree with Raz that we should not be looking for new forms of natural law theory in order to save "universal morality" as an instrument of the critique of positive law. There exists no natural universal morality that can serve as a pre-given morality for social orders to follow. A critical analysis of concrete forms of social cooperation is all we can hope for and all we need.

However, this does not mean that we are justified in rejecting the criterion of universalizability of valid moral judgments. Contextual forms of injustices, including unjust legal norms, become transparent when subjected to the criterion of universalizability. In its critical form, this criterion has nothing to do with the idea of a uniform universal morality. In order to satisfy the criterion of universalizability a moral judgment need not be binding in every time and space. Instead, a universalizable moral judgment is binding when applied to significantly similar situations. Richard Hare offers the most critically potent reading of universalizability:

> Universalizability can be explained in various equivalent ways; it comes to this, that if we make different moral judgments about situations which we admit to be identical in their universal descriptive properties, we contradict ourselves.[62]

The key here is that Hare discriminates between moral judgments of a general character and those that can be universalized. Universalism of natural law tends to focus on general principles and values that are uniformly applicable in all contexts. Reason or some other dimension of humanity is seen as a foundation for such justification. In Hare, concrete social contexts and situations impose special demands on moral judgments. Such judgments are particular rather than general, and we are expected to reason in a similar fashion when situations are identical.

When applied to social norms that aspire to moral legitimacy, Hare's version of universalism means that we need not look for universal *ideals* to justify such norms. What we do need is to investigate whether our moral judgments can be universalized for all identical situations. Let us take human rights as an example. From the perspective of natural law theory, human rights regulations are universal because they secure respect for human dignity. This dignity is the same for all humanity, which means that human rights should be essentially uniform. In practice, dominant traditions tend to present their particular understandings of dignity and rights as universally valid. This is especially common among human rights defenders who identify liberal and post-Christian understandings of human rights as *the* genuine protection of human dignity. Such an identification, even if based on the best possible motives, suppresses alternative traditions and becomes an ideology of domination rather than an instrument of critique and liberation.

The criterion of universalizability that I am defending does not presuppose a belief in universal humanity in any essentialist sense. Nor does it presuppose the existence of a universally valid moral law that human rights regulations must incorporate. The content of treating people in a dignified or undignified way can vary depending on the time and context. However, when we exercise our moral judgment to argue for a particular interpretation or prioritizing of human rights, we are not allowed to judge identical situations differently.

The prohibition of discrimination is thus the most important justificatory test of human rights regulations. Human rights as posited law is not morally justified if it peacefully coexists with discrimination. This is already recognized in most human rights conventions that make the prohibition of discrimination fundamental to the proper implementation of universal human rights. For example, there are reasonable disagreements on the exact meaning of freedom of speech. However, for a state to grant this right (interpreted in a particular context) to some while refusing it to others is a violation of human dignity.

Although I endorse Hare's principle of universalizability, I am skeptical toward his understanding of the agency of moral critique. In my view, the democratic agency of the unprivileged is a fundamental requirement if discriminatory judgments and practices are to be made visible. I therefore disagree with Hare, who believed that philosophical reasoning is the most effective tool for exposing self-contradictions in the use of moral judgment. On the contrary, the formal demand for universalizability of valid moral judgments is critical when it is invoked by those whose material conditions ral judgment of the privileged seem self-contradictory. Those ted to racism, exploitation, and patriarchy *experience* the con- n official ideologies of "equal human rights." In many cases, this experience devalues the very idea of human rights.[63] However, another and far more productive way of dealing with ideological repurposings of the concept of human rights (as well as other ideals of political morality) is to demand changes in human rights law on the basis of lived experiences of legally protected injustice. This demand, though expressed in moral terms, can only ever be political in nature.

To sum up, the critical potential of Raz's legal positivism as a theory of law and morality is weakened by his endorsement of a liberal moral "doctrine" that he interprets through the lens of a modified Aristotelian ethics. In order to fully use the critical resources of legal positivism, we need to combine the separation thesis, which Raz rightly links to the law's claim to legitimate authority, with another type of political ethics. This ethics should be able to offer instruments for a critique of positive norms by exposing social injustice, which is both a moral issue and an object for political struggle. Such a struggle is a crucial part of the politics that Raz underestimates by defining the law as an instrument of social cooperation.

## NOTES

1. Joseph Raz, *Between Authority and Interpretation. On the Theory of Law and Practical Reason* (Oxford, UK: Oxford University Press, 2009), 180.
2. Joseph Raz, *Practical Reason and Norms* (Oxford, UK: Oxford University Press, 1975), 163–169.
3. Joseph Raz, *The Authority of Law*. Second edition (Oxford, UK: Oxford University Press, 2009), 158.
4. Raz, *Between Authority and Interpretation*, 101.
5. Ibid., 119.
6. Raz, *Practical Reason and Norms*, 143.
7. Ibid., 145.
8. Ibid., 145.
9. Ibid., 135.
10. Ibid., 151.
11. Raz, *The Authority of Law*, 134.
12. Ibid., 134.
13. Ibid., 137.
14. Joseph Raz, *Engaging Reason. On the Theory of Value and Action* (Oxford, UK: Oxford University Press, 1999), 68.
15. Ibid., 70.
16. Raz, *Between Authority and Interpretation*, 128–129.
17. See Shivprasad Swaminathan, "Projectivism and the Metaethical Foundations of the Normativity of Law," *Jurisprudence* 7, no. 2 (2016): 231–266.
18. Raz, *Engaging Reason*, 87.
19. Ibid., 75.

20. Raz, *The Authority of Law*, 253.
21. Ibid., 167.
22. Ibid., 176.
23. Ibid., 249.
24. Raz, *Between Authority and Interpretation*, 101.
25. Raz, *The Authority of Law*, 249.
26. Raz, *Between Authority and Interpretation*, 180.
27. Raz, *The Authority of Law*, 316.
28. Raz, *Practical Reason and Norms,* 193.
29. Raz, *Between Authority and Interpretation*, 135.
30. Ibid., 136–137.
31. Ibid., 139.
32. Ibid., 189.
33. Joseph Raz, *The Morality of Freedom* (Oxford, UK: Oxford Scholarship Online, 2003 (1988)), 5.
34. Ibid., 3.
35. Ibid., 193–194.
36. Ibid., 198.
37. Here I use the term ideology in a more conventional sense, i.e. as a system of normative convictions about human beings, society, and political morality.
38. Raz, *The Morality of Freedom*, 400. My emphasis.
39. Ibid., 372–373.
40. Ibid., 408.
41. Ibid., 425.
42. Ibid., 426–427.
43. Ibid., 427.
44. Raz, *Engaging Reason*, 179.
45. Raz, *The Morality of Freedom*, 261.
46. Ibid., 263 (footnote).
47. Raz, *Between Authority and Interpretation,* 119.
48. I agree with Raz when he describes Rawls theory as an attempt to offer an operational theory. In the first paragraph in *A Theory of Justice*, Rawls states that his theory is an alternative to utilitarian and intuitionist *doctrines*. John Rawls, *A Theory of Justice* (Oxford, UK: Oxford University Press, 1972), 3.
49. For a nuanced critique of the liberal moralism, see Carl-Henric Grenholm, *Kritisk politisk etik. Om moralens betydelse inom politiken* (Uppsala: Acta Universitatis Upsaliensis, 2024), 185–222.
50. Raz, *Engaging Reason*, 86.
51. For discussions on political cultures as traditions, see, for example, Jeffrey Stout, *Democracy and Tradition* (Princeton, NJ: Princeton University Press, 2004); Cécile Laborde, *Critical Republicanism* (Oxford, UK: Oxford University Press, 2008); Michael Walzer, *The Paradox of Liberation* (New Haven, CT: Yale University Press, 2017).
52. Raz, *The Morality of Freedom*, 254.
53. Ibid., 254.

54. In this particular context, Raz endorses what I have described as epistemological legal positivism. He regards the factual practices in the domain of international law as the exclusive object of scientific inquiry.

55. Joseph Raz, "Human Rights without foundations," in *The Philosophy of International Law*, eds. Samantha Besson and John Tasioulas (Oxford, UK: Oxford University Press, 2010), 328.

56. Ibid., 331.

57. Ibid., 321.

58. It must be acknowledged that this analysis is offered by Raz in the context of an anthology on international law. However, it is revealing that as late as in 2010 he still does not mention the political dimension of human rights.

59. Joseph Raz, "Disagreement in Politics," *American Journal of Jurisprudence* 43 (1998): 52.

60. Ibid., 48.

61. This seems to be confirmed at least in the cases of Nazi Germany and Stalin's Soviets. In their description of Nazi dictatorship, Franz Neumann, Herbert Marcuse, and Felix Gilbert state that German "society has been completely pulverized into its individual atoms which are then organized and manipulated from the top down." *Secret Reports on Nazi Germany. The Frankfurt School Contribution to the War Effort*, ed. Raffaele Laudani (Princeton, NJ: Princeton University Press, 2013), 108.

62. Richard Hare, *Moral Thinking. Its Levels, Method and Point* (Oxford, UK: Clarendon Press, 1981), 21.

63. For example, many postcolonial activists and political theorists are skeptical of human rights because, as they rightly argue, these rights have been efficiently used as colonialist ideology. See Balakrishnan Rajagopal, *International Law from Bellow. Development, Social Movements and Third World Resistance* (Cambridge, UK: Cambridge University Press, 2003).

# Chapter 5

# Jürgen Habermas

## *Democracy and the Law*

> Modern law is formed by a system of norms that are coercive, positive, and, so it claimed, freedom-guaranteeing.[1]

In this chapter, I interpret and scrutinize Habermas's understanding of the law and its relationship to politics and morality. For obvious reasons, my aim is not to offer a comprehensive presentation of Habermas's work. Rather, I focus on some fundamental elements of his interpretation of the facticity and normativity of the law as they appear in *Between Facts and Norms. Contributions to a Discourse Theory of Law and Democracy.*

There are a number of reasonable interpretations of *Between Facts and Norms*, each with its corresponding critical approach. While some scholars look for theoretical resources of a sociological nature in order to grasp contemporary developments, others are primarily interested in the conceptual scheme of Habermas's seminal work on modern law and democracy. The reading proposed here takes critical theory as its starting point, which means that I interpret Habermas's theory of law, politics, and morality as a critique of different forms of injustice and democratic deficit rather than as a normative vision of the democracy and its law. At the same time, I do not believe that Habermas's descriptive analysis of historical and contemporary developments is the most valuable aspect of his thinking, precisely because Habermas reduces his investigation of contemporary capitalism to an analysis of Western European and North American societies.

My choice of critical theory as my main interpretative perspective depends on the design of this particular investigation as well as on Habermas's own belief that the philosopher should strive to contribute to the philosophical analysis of justification and valid forms of practical judgments rather than arguing for or against particular normative positions. The "moral point of view," which Habermas believes ought to be explained by the philosopher, is bound up with the universality claim that in practice subjects any substantial position or particular practice to scrutiny.[2]

Those who read Habermas differently—for example, by seeking to make his theory applicable beyond the fundamental critique of social institutions such as law and state[3]—rely on the ambivalence that is explicitly present and addressed in his work, above all in *Between Facts and Norms*, which deals with both the facticity and the normativity of the law. Habermas wants us to join him in a dialectical understanding of the relationship between the positivity of law and its legitimacy. This is an onerous request, which explains why many commentators expect Habermas to approach particular legal dimensions of democracy and envision alternatives. In my view, the most generous reading of the theory of deliberative democracy and modern law does not treat it as a normative project akin to Rawls's political liberalism. Nor is it productive to read *Between Facts and Norms* as a traditional philosophical theory of law (the monograph does not even address specific issues of legal philosophy in a reasonably nuanced manner). Instead, Habermas's analysis of law and democracy is a highly abstract theory about the relationship between modern law, politics, and morality, which allows us to critique different kinds of democratic deficit in the current stage of capitalism.

How then does Habermas's understanding of the relationship between law, politics, and morality become a resource for the social critique of legal regulations? What are the limitations of his approach? What role does "the moral point of view" play in *Between Facts and Norms*? In order to address these questions, I first discuss Habermas's understanding of the dialectics of facticity and legitimacy in modern law. I begin with his use of different types of rights as a scheme for the dialectics of private and political autonomy. Next, I interpret and scrutinize Habermas's attempt to overcome the dichotomy between natural law and legal positivism. Finally, I discuss the elements of Habermas's theory of law and democracy that variously strengthen and weaken its critical potential.

## RIGHTS AND LAW

In *Between Facts and Norms*, Habermas offers a discourse-theoretical approach to the issue of the legitimacy of modern law. As his postscript to the volume states:

> Modern law is formed by a system of norms that are coercive, positive, and, so it claimed, freedom-guaranteeing. The formal properties of coercion and positivity are associated with the claim to legitimacy: the fact that norms backed

> by the threat of state sanction stem from the changeable decisions of a political lawgiver is linked with the expectation that these norms guarantee the autonomy of all legal persons equally.[4]

The phrase "[equal] autonomy of all legal persons" indicates that Habermas explicitly theorizes law, politics, and morality within modern Western culture. Self-legislation is the most important form of subjectivity and freedom that Habermas assigns to the modern project of political, personal, and social emancipation. Habermas even describes "the idea of autonomy according to which human beings act as free subjects only insofar as they obey just those laws they give themselves in accordance with insights they have acquired intersubjectively" as the *dogmatic core* of his interpretation of constitutionalism and the rule of law.[5]

Furthermore, and most importantly, Habermas defends the rationalism of the European Enlightenment against its critics on both the right and the left. His understanding of the law and democratic politics stands in sharp contrast to Carl Schmitt's philosophy "according to which 'the political' consists merely in the self-assertion of a collective identity over against other collective identities."[6]

How does Habermas understand modern law—both its positivity and legitimacy? To begin with, he approaches the issue of the positivity and legitimacy of modern law dialectically rather than analytically. Instead of searching for a satisfactory definition of the law, he offers an account of how concepts of law, politics, and morality are interrelated in a particular historical context. The character of the positivity of modern law, he claims, is linked to—"associated," "intertwined with"—a particular form of legitimacy, and vice versa. Unlike Hart and Raz, who agree that the law can be conceptualized trans-contextually, Habermas focuses on the law of Western modernity, which, he argues, is characterized by a specific dialectic of positivity and legitimacy. The changeable decisions of political legislators, he claims, are the only source of legal norms. Simultaneously, they are expected to guarantee equal autonomy. Clearly, there is something about the nature of political decision-making in modern democracy that justifies the expectation that the equal autonomy of all persons can be secured by positive law.

According to Habermas, it is democratic constitutionalism, that is, popular sovereignty into which a particular system of rights has been incorporated, that ensures (or should ensure) that the legitimacy of positive law is linked to the expectation of equal autonomy.

The principle of the constitutional state is described by Habermas as follows:

> the organization of the constitutional state is ultimately supposed to serve the politically autonomous self-organization of a community that has constituted

> itself with the system of rights as an association of free and equal consociates under law. The institutions of the constitutional state are supposed to secure an effective exercise of the political autonomy of socially autonomous citizens.[7]

Thus, rights are understood by Habermas as an incarnation of the dialectics of positivity and legitimacy of law, which in turn is a form of the dialectics of facticity and validity of social norms. Democratic sovereignty demands the preservation of the tension between the facticity and the legitimacy of law. Precisely because this tension cannot be definitely resolved, rights do not transcend the tension (as they do in the natural law tradition) but operationalize it:

> [Positivity and legitimacy of law] combine in the mutual penetration of legal form and discourse principle [i.e. the principle stipulating that for norms to be valid they should meet with approval of all affected as participants in a practical discourse], as well as in the Janus faces that law turns toward its addresses on the one side and its authors on the other. On the one side, by way of coercible laws that render equal liberties compatible, the system of rights unleashes the self-interested choice of individual subjects oriented by personal preferences. On the other side, in the practice of legislation, it mobilizes and unifies the communicative freedom of citizens presumptively oriented to the common good.[8]

It is crucial that fundamental rights in a constitutional democracy[9] are not treated as natural—if by "natural" we mean an abstract and ideal (or, in Habermas terminology, Platonic) morality that is expected to be realized by means of politics and law. There are no universally legitimate or *in abstracto* justified norms; there is no natural law beyond positive legal norms. The same law comprises a dialectics of both positivity and legitimacy, and it does so contextually. In modern democracy, rights bind together the positivity of legal norms, as it appears to the addressees and subjects of legal implementations, with the legitimacy of legal norms as manifested in the necessarily contextual practices of legislation.

Already in his "Natural Law and Revolution" published in English translation in 1974, Habermas introduced his understanding of fundamental rights as a particular modern construction. At that point, Habermas formed his view of fundamental rights as a critique of Karl Marx's famous reading of bourgeois (political) rights as "the emancipation of citizens but not of human beings."[10] Habermas's interpretation of Marxian theory of fundamental rights is reasonably questioned by scholars.[11] However, regardless the obvious lack of accuracy in the very reading of Marx, Habermas was looking for a concept of fundamental rights that connects rights as "the principles of a constitution organizing society and the state" with liberal rights protecting private persons from the "interventions and usurpations by the state."[12]

In *Between Facts and Norms*, we find an ambitious scheme of rights that Habermas presents as a rational reconstruction of the self-understanding of modern legal orders.[13] This means that Habermas's interpretation of fundamental rights as securing both private liberties and civic autonomy in modern democracy is still a critical project. In other words, Habermas's reconstruction of different types of basic and interrelated rights is less a descriptive analysis of concrete practices in the legal protection of rights than a philosophical transcription of a particular kind of democratic constitutionalism as it appears to politically active citizens.[14] As noted earlier, I see the main aim of such a construction as being to provide an instrument for the social critique of institutions—including legal institutions—within the paradigm of constitutional democracy.

Habermas reconstructs three abstract categories of basic rights, which he also presents as legal principles. This reconstruction presupposes that the modern legal form of social norms is combined with the legitimacy of such norms that can be tested in light of the discourse principle.[15] This principle depicts valid justification of norms as "the approval [or possible approval] of all affected in their capacity *as participants in a practical discourse*."[16]

The dialectical relationship between legal form and discursive legitimization of norms is thus crucial for constitutional democracy. As Habermas explains in "Remarks on Discourse Ethics":

> The idea of the constitutional state can then be understood in terms of the endeavor to institutionalize the demanding communicative presuppositions and procedures of a network of forms of argumentation and negotiation differentiated in terms of the problem areas, for the political power employed in executing the requirements of the principle of discourse must itself be tamed through discourse.[17]

Basic rights (i.e., constitutional rights as reconstructed by Habermas) regulate relationships among freely associated citizens and consist of: (1) the right to the greatest possible measure of equal individual liberty; (2) the right to have the status of a member in a voluntary association; and (3) the right to legal protection. All of these rights are the result of politically autonomous elaboration and should not be viewed as moral foundations of the law that must be respected by the state.[18] By means of these basic rights, legal subjects recognize each other as rights holders—that is, as addressees of the law.

In the next and crucial step of his reconstruction, Habermas introduces "basic rights to equal opportunities to participate in processes of opinion- and will-formation in which citizens exercise their *political autonomy* and through which they generate legitimate law."[19] Precisely this category of rights (which demands social rights in order to be practiced) creates citizens as the subject—the author—of law. Only through such a law—that is, a law aiming at preserving communicative spheres for opinion- and will-formation—do traditional (liberal) human rights[20] come into existence. Thus, human rights in the conventional sense, not least as articulated in international human rights treaties, are not the starting point of Habermas's reconstruction. Rather, human rights—if such exist—are derivative of the basic rights that citizens grant each other.

Habermas's scheme of basic rights seeks to demonstrate how popular sovereignty and human rights are mutually constitutive. Human rights are not pre-given by some kind of natural morality. Nor are they the product of enlightened monological reason. Only equal citizens who are simultaneously the subjects of legislation and the objects of law can create the "foundation" of legally granted human rights, something that is achieved by means of practical deliberation, itself regulated in turn by law. In modernity, the very process of legislation (democratic will-formation) is thus mediated by legal norms.

According to Habermas, "a system of rights that brings private and public autonomy into a relation of mutual presupposition" is the result of an interpenetration of the discourse principle and the legal medium.[21] Let us recall that the discourse principle is a meta-principle of the discourse ethics that both presupposes "that normative claims to validity have cognitive meaning and [. . .] that the justification of norms and commands requires that a real discourse be carried out."[22] The principle of discourse ethics states: "Only those norms can claim to be valid that meet (or could meet) with the approval of all affected in their capacity *as participants in a practical discourse*."[23]

This principle is a principle of justification: it offers a general form of valid practical judgment. Formal as it appears, the principle should be applied to practical democratic discourse, that is, complex deliberations on behalf of political agents. Such deliberations have several dimensions among which moral and institutional are crucial.

In order for norms to be morally valid, the argumentation within practical discourse should fulfill the criterion of universalization. According to Habermas, the principle of universalization states: "every valid norm has to fulfill the following condition: *All* affected can accept the consequences and the side effects its *general* observance can be anticipated to have for the satisfaction of *everyone's* interests."[24] In *Between Facts and Norms*, Habermas highlights the fact that "the moral principle functions as a rule of argumentation for deciding moral questions rationally."[25]

Enabling democratic and rational opinion- and will-formation calls for yet another principle, namely the institutionalization of practical discourse. The "moral principle," that is, universalization principle, offers the criterion for normative validity, while the principle of democracy stipulates that rational will-formation should be institutionalized "through a system of rights that secures for each person an equal participation in a process of legislation whose communicative presuppositions are guaranteed to begin with."[26] Basic rights are thus the legal medium of institutionalized democratic will-formation. Simultaneously and in their different concrete forms, rights—including human rights—are constructed through this deliberative will-formation.

Comparison with Hart highlights the particular character of Habermas's interpretation of basic rights. As we have seen, Hart understands the moral justification of legal norms as a theoretical enterprise and dismisses the deontological theory of rights in favor of utilitarian normative theory. Most importantly, Hart finds it difficult to use abstract human rights as a tool for the moral justification of law in a democracy. The reason why is that he regards all theories of rights as based upon a theory of *natural moral duties* on behalf of the state. Hart thus worries—rightly so, I would say—that the state's duty as a moral foundation of human rights can easily be combined with anti-democratic state paternalism. Rights are regarded as being granted to citizens by a state that recognizes its moral obligations toward the objects of its "care." As a result, citizens are not agents of power but its addressees.

Habermas understands both the justification of legal norms and the meaning of rights differently and therefore presents rights as constitutive of the modern legal system and *democracy*. In Habermas's reconstruction, not only do basic rights enable a democratic legislation that maintains a connection with communicative practices, but rights themselves are simultaneously the products of such a legislation. Rights, both as constructed through collective will-formation and as constitutive for such a formation, are part of constitutional self-understanding, a unique model of social cooperation that treats objects of the law as subjects of the same changeable law.

Even for Habermas, the moral language of rights is deontological and therefore includes the category of universalizable duties. Yet, these are not the "natural duties" of the state toward citizens but, rather, the products of political agency on behalf of citizens. As we have seen, "the self-understanding of constitutional democracy" is the theoretical reconstruction of a view of active citizens as utilizing constitutional principles in political practice. The deliberative character of democratic politics is sustained and developed by the functionality of constitutional principles (democracy's own self-understanding), such as the principle of equal respect for human dignity that we will discuss later.

## BEYOND NATURAL LAW

Habermas is explicit in his ambition to get rid of remains from the natural law tradition which he characterizes as a form of Platonism whose "doubling

[of] law into natural and positive law suggests that historical legal orders are supposed to *copy* a pregiven suprasensible order."[27] In both Kant and Rawls, Habermas finds a type of social contract theory that still includes elements of the Platonism of natural law. Although social contract theory has a different metaphysics from that of the classical tradition of natural law, its view of rationality is nonetheless marked by the idealism of natural law tradition. Habermas's critique of the original position and the theory of reflective equilibrium[28] is mainly a critique of Rawls's (and Kant's) particular understanding of practical reason. This reason operates *in abstracto* and simultaneously aspires to offer direct guidance for human action in the political and social sphere.

The fairness of Habermas's critique of the elements of natural law in Rawls is an open question. What matters here is Habermas's aim of entirely abandoning a transcendent reason that aspires for direct applicability to human actions and institutions. Communicative reason is supposed to do this job by opening up "postmetaphysical thinking" in practical philosophy.[29] The key here is the fact that communicative reason and its validity claims are immanent to human cooperation through language. Validity claims can only be justified discursively: there are neither moral nor legal norms whose validity can be tested outside actual discursive practices. This is why "the moral principle" in Habermas's theory is a rule of *argumentation*—that is, moral argumentation within the democratic discourse.

What, then, is the relationship between morality and law, according to Habermas? In *Between Facts and Norms*, he argues for a complementary relationship between morality and positive law. This complementarity is a defining feature of post-traditional (modern) society and, according to Habermas, appears in several forms. To begin with, both morality and law refer to the same problems of social cooperation, but differently. While morality is a form of practical knowledge, law operates on a binding institutional level.[30]

Furthermore, the principle of justification of social norms—the discourse principle—is neutral in relation to morality and law. The discourse principle presupposes that practical questions on both moral and institutional levels can be decided rationally. Moral norms are justified discursively in accordance with the universalization principle and legal norms are justified in accordance with the democratic principle. This principle states that "only those statutes may claim legitimacy that can meet with the assent (*Zustimmung*) of all citizens in a discursive process of legislation."[31]

A good example of the complementarity between law and morality is how human rights appear in morality and law respectively. Only in law can moral rights take the form of subjective rights, that is, rights that can be legitimately claimed (legitimate legal norms) and firmly granted (posited legal norms). In an article on human rights and constitutionalism published in 2010, Habermas follows Luhmann in explaining that the same rights are both moral and legal. Moral rights are valid through the justification of moral duties and legal rights by being part of a legitimate legal order. In Habermas's words:

> A person in a *moral relation* asks herself what she owes to another person independently of her social relation to him—how well she knows him, how he behaves, and what she might expect of him. People who stand in a *legal relation* to one another are concerned about potential *claims* they expect others to make on them. In a legal community, the first person acquires obligation as a result of claims that a second person makes on her.[32]

The principle of democracy thus "presupposes the possibility of moral judgments"[33] while also defining the justification of such social norms that appear in legal form. The particular form of legal norms (positivity, the institutional character of their enforcement), rather than their substance, accounts for why the justification of legal norms differs from the justification of moral norms.

It is crucial for Habermas that morality should not be reduced to the regulation of social relationships for which we have personal responsibility. There is no difference between law and morality in regard to the fact that both also regulate the public sphere. It is therefore impossible to distinguish between moral and legal norms on the basis of their substance.

Morality and law are thus both essentially normative regulators of social relations. However, legal and moral norms take different forms. According to Habermas, only legal norms appear in a positive form. Morality is a domain of obligation that lays claim to universality while law is the domain of claims that people expect to be reciprocally respected. While the claim to validity made by moral norms may be obvious, legal norms also aspire for normative validity and are therefore in need of justification. Importantly, the justification of legal norms includes pragmatic, ethical-political, and moral reasons. While the criteria of moral justification are entirely rational, legal norms are valid as a result of combining normative validity with factual social acceptance.

In my interpretation of Habermas, both the moral principle and the democratic principle of argumentation are critical in nature. His claim that the discourse principle "presupposes" rational deliberation does not mean that such deliberation is actually taking place in contemporary democracies. What it does mean is that a particular normative self-understanding of deliberative democracy—reconstructed in the principle of discourse ethics and its two "incarnations"—has the potential to uncover democratic deficits, unjustified political norms, and illegitimate statutes, thereby contributing to the political critique of factual social norms and institutions.

Where does this leave us with regard to Habermas's position on natural law and legal positivism? Natural moral law is not the foundation of the legitimacy of legal norms, but nor is factual power (to legislate and enforce the law). Legitimate legal norms are posited norms that have been institutionalized according to the democratic principle. Legitimate legal norms in this strong sense are immanent to the claim to legitimacy that belongs to modern democracy's "self-understanding." Habermas's theory of the dialectical relationship between positive legal norms and their normative justification is thus a critical theory and not a description of legal orders that *are* legitimate. Habermas differs from natural law theorists in that he rejects the existence of universally valid substantial morality. Nor does he endorse the kind of legal positivism that identifies the legitimacy of legal norms with the social legitimacy of legislative power.

In my reading, one particular move by Habermas, namely his reconstruction of modern democracy's self-understanding, situates his approach to normativity in law within the variety of legal positivism introduced by Hart. Both Hart and Habermas, albeit in different ways, view the law's claim to moral legitimacy as a source of politically powerful critique and thus as a resource for the development of legal systems.

Habermas's conception of the complementarity of law and morality means that legal norms "claim to *be in accord* with moral norms, that is not to violate them" even as they can simultaneously "be justified not only with moral but also with pragmatic and ethical-political reasons."[34] Such a dialectical relationship between moral and legal validity presupposes a firm rejection of the objective substantial morality. The moral norms that legitimate legal norms claim to be in agreement with are themselves products of social construction: they do not exist beyond social discourses.

Valid moral norms—those with which legitimate legal norms claim to be in accordance—should be justified discursively in light of the universalization principle. What kind of norms does Habermas have in mind? A good candidate for such a norm is the principle of equal respect for human dignity.[35] This *moral* principle is legitimately constitutional because it passes the test of discursive universalization. The argument in support of this thesis is that violations of human dignity that appear in different contextual forms (humiliation, oppression, etc.) are the basis upon which both the moral universal duty to respect each individual's human dignity and the subjective right of each individual to be recognized as equally human rest. On a moral level, it is reasonable to argue in favor of universal responsibility as a way to respect each and everyone's humanity. However, a particular political and legal structure is required in order to secure the equal social status of all individuals (respect for human dignity) in terms of subjective rights. Human rights in modern political history, Habermas states, spell out the normative substance of every human being's equal dignity.[36] Yet, they do so by means of positive law, a particular *form* of normativity: human rights are not *the* implementation of a universal moral law. Whenever they exist, they do so as the result of political struggle for equal social standing on behalf of the underprivileged. Yet, this struggle is discursively justifiable, or so Habermas claims.

Accordingly, enforcing the moral principle of respect for human dignity—through particular cultures of rights in different modern societies—can only be the result of moral, ethical-political, and pragmatic argumentation. Moral principles are always abstract and, as we have seen, are phenomenologically a matter of universalized duty, which means that the moral principle of equal respect for human dignity cannot be incorporated into positive law without changing its form. The medium of the law transforms the principle from its moral form into the form of subjective rights that citizens grant each other as legislators. For this very reason, Habermas therefore emphasizes that human dignity is a constitutional principle:

> *human dignity forms the "portal" through which the egalitarian and universalistic substance of morality is imported into law.* The idea of human dignity is the conceptual hinge that connects the *morality* of equal respect for everyone with positive *law* and democratic lawmaking in such a way that their interplay could give rise to a political order founded upon human rights.[37]

Equal respect for human dignity is "the portal," Habermas argues, placing emphasis on this particular wording. Already in its constitutional form, the moral principle is transformed by its legal form, and as a constitutional principle it comprises a tension between the moral view of equality and social equality that can be secured by the medium of law. The tension between the moral ideal of equal human dignity and rights in their legal form is not something Habermas wants us to resolve. Rather, he understands this tension as crucial for sustaining the "utopian gap" that enables progressive democratic politics.

This utopian gap between the moral ideal of equality and equality as constructed by systems of rights differs from the social utopia of human rights as articulated in terms of natural law. In my reading, it is crucial that Habermas distances himself from the understandings of human rights, which allow for the existence of a uniform system of human rights that is positively formulated and firmly enforced (as, for example, in international treaties). Theoretically, such views disregard the tension between the legal form of rights and their moral justification. At the same time, they tend to legitimize inequality between peoples and the lack of democracy at the global level.[38] According to Habermas, a moral utopia of human rights is realistic if, and only if, it is coupled with sovereign democratic legislation—that is, with the social construction of subjective rights.

Habermas's approach to human rights has been further clarified by Rainer Forst. In his theory of human rights, Forst defends the classical approach to state sovereignty and human rights against the idea that human rights regulations in all states should be subordinated to a single international authority (e.g., a strong judicial review and executive power wielded on behalf of the United Nations). While the desire for such a subordination is understandable, it overlooks the crucial importance of a justificatory practice that can be exercised only within sovereign political communities. Imperfect as social norms in an unjust world inevitably are, human rights—if interpreted and implemented by means of self-legislation in sovereign states—do not lose their crucial connectedness to the political autonomy of individuals and peoples.[39]

The examples presented by human rights and the constitutional principle of equal respect for human dignity make it clear that Habermas, in fact, rejects the natural law approach on two counts—fundamentally, on the moral level, but also as applied to the issue of the moral legitimacy of positive law. First, no objective moral law exists that transcends social norms in particular social contexts. Habermas rejects both the traditional Christian and the rationalistic post-Christian metaphysics of natural law. Second, morality (in modernity) is entirely a matter of justification: there is no such a thing as universally valid substantial morality. There are, therefore, no *objective* substantial norms that might be invoked to either confirm or problematize the legitimacy of posited norms.

Morality and law are dialectically related to each other and both are immanent to the social norms of particular societies. This means that morality and law are constructed and challenge each other in particular social and linguistic contexts. Human rights, for instance, nowhere exist as substantially moral norms that transcend the moral, ethical-political, and pragmatic discourses of different societies.

## BEYOND LEGAL POSITIVISM?

In *Between Facts and Norms*, Habermas himself states that his firm rejection of natural law is not an embracing of legal positivism. The claim makes its appearance when Habermas discusses Ronald Dworkin's critique of legal positivism. In that context, Habermas states that the dichotomy between natural law and positivism is resolved in his own theory of law and democracy. Let us look at the statement more closely.

Habermas presents his position on the issue of legal validity and moral legitimacy as similar to that of Dworkin, whose interpretation and critique of legal positivism he shares:

> Dworkin's theory of rights is premised on the claim that moral arguments play a role in adjudication because positive law has unavoidably absorbed a moral content. This premise harbors no surprise for a discourse theory starting with the assumption that moral reasons enter into law via democratic procedure of legislation (and through the fairness conditions of compromise formation).[40]

As already noted, Dworkin treats legal theory "as a special part of political morality distinguished by a further refinement of institutional structures."[41] Furthermore, Dworkin regards human rights (which in his theory are reconstructed from the Constitution of the United States) as crucial for the relationship between law and morality in a modern democracy. The main guardian of human rights is, or should be, the lawyer. The ideal judge in Dworkin's interpretative theory of law adjudicates by harmonizing his interpretation of positive statues with constitutional rights, which are, in turn, understood in the light of the moral-political principle of equal respect and concern. Such adjudication provides, according to Dworkin, "the best interpretation of the other propositions of law generally treated as true in contemporary legal practice."[42]

Habermas endorses the idea that moral content is "absorbed" in positive law. There is no moral law outside social norms, and legal norms are fundamentally important social norms in modern society. However, Habermas overestimates the similarities between Dworkin's anti-positivism and his own view on law, morality, and politics. As I see it, Habermas's theory differs from Dworkin's in regard to how the moral justification of legal norms is understood. In short, Dworkin believes that the legal interpretations which "flow from principles of personal and political morality" are "true propositions of law." This means that there is always one true interpretation of law in hard cases. Dworkin's hypothetical super-judge Hercules arrives at such true legal propositions by grounding his adjudication on *the* moral meaning of constitutional principles and human rights.

Dworkin's reconstruction of the moral dimension of positive law is thus monologically rationalistic[43] and static when contrasted to that of Habermas. According to Habermas, democratic and discursive will-formation—as opposed to the reasoning of a hypothetical judge (Dworkin's Hercules)—is the source of the moral content of the fundamental rights that take a particular legal form in modernity. While Dworkin believes that within the American Constitution there exists such a thing as the true moral meaning of human rights to be defended by the lawyer, Habermas understands the constitutions of democratic societies as ongoing democratic enterprises.

Habermas does not regard valid moral norms as exclusively and substantially valid, that is, as "true." In his explanation of the moral language, validity in the context of moral normativity is *an analogy* to propositional truth.[44]

Most importantly, there are no objectively valid substantial moral norms to be found in any existing constitutional document. Valid moral norms are *constituted* through the very practice of justification, and such a discursive practice cannot be finalized. Additionally, Habermas is consistent in how he describes the normative quality of legal norms in terms of legality and legitimacy, rather than, as Dworkin does, in terms of "true propositions of law." For Habermas, morally justified legal norms are constructed through particular types of discourse, not determined by a substantial morality that is transcendent to the discourse itself.

Despite the significant differences between their respective understandings of political morality, Habermas endorses Dworkin's antagonistic presentation of legal positivism, especially that of Hart.[45] Why is that? In my view, Habermas is simply unaware of the fact that Dworkin persistently disregards one crucial element of Hart's theory of law and morality: its focus on the practice of legislation, rather than adjudication. While Dworkin reads Hart as a theorist of adjudication, Hart is explicitly interested in the moral quality of law as a result of democratic legislation. According to Hart, immoral *and* legally valid norms motivate the democratic political agency of citizens and politicians. Immoral legal norms should be changed politically. They cannot be morally corrected by the reasoning of a super-judge. I believe that Habermas in fact shares Hart's view of legislation and therefore of democratic will-formation as constitutive of the moral dimension of law.

Let us recall that Habermas's idea that the coercive law's aspiration to protect freedom has to do with modern democracy's "self-understanding." The value of freedom is not secured by its being inscribed in the founding documents of a modern democracy. Rather, freedom is something that politically active citizens constitute by engaging in a struggle for the meaning of freedom. While Dworkin finds morality of freedom in the American Constitution, Habermas is not interested in offering *a list* of morally justified legal principles. The moral validity of legal principles and norms are essentially discursive, future-oriented, and therefore immanent to political practices. In Habermas, as in Hart, legally valid norms *are not* necessarily morally valid norms. Dworkin's position is different and lies closer to Rawls's liberal moralism. Both philosophers view the United States Constitution as including universally valid substantial moral principles and rights.

What can we now say about Habermas's explicitly stated belief that his interpretation of positivity and legitimacy as dialectically related dimensions of one and the same law transcends the traditional dichotomy of natural law and legal positivism? Is he right?

Habermas does indeed adopt a radical position in rejecting the existence of two kinds of law, which in practice means that he rejects the existence of natural law—universal moral law as the model for legitimate positive law

Most importantly, Habermas rejects the "normativism" of natural law, that is, any attempt to find the content of practical reason in either the teleology of history or human nature.[46] As we saw in the example offered by Habermas's understanding of human dignity, while this *moral principle* stipulates that humanity of each and every one should be respected equally, it says nothing about the substance of such a respect. Nor does it describe what humanity is. This is so because the substance of equal respect for humanity is immanent to social practice and can only come into existence through practical discourses.

In my view, it is the democratic pathos of Habermas's philosophical project that prevents him from endorsing natural law. Natural law is anti-democratic because it tempts us to look for objectively valid principles and norms that should be incorporated in *lex humana*. In Habermas, practical reason is social and communicative. It constitutes rather than discovers valid normative judgments. Communicative reason does not "contain" substantial normativity, as is highlighted by Habermas in his principle of universalization as exclusively a rule of rational argumentation. Moral validity is immanent to justified legal norms, while, at the same time, legally valid norms are not necessarily morally valid.

Habermas believes that the moral scrutiny of legal norms is crucial for the progressive development of democratic legal systems. To raise the question of moral validity (legitimacy) with regard to positive law is not just possible; it is an essential element of the modern democratic project that a theory of law, morality, and politics should address.

From the above discussion, I conclude that Habermas's theory of law and morality does not "transcend" the dichotomy of natural law and positivism. The main advantage of his theory is, rather, its dialectical approach to the positivity and legitimacy of social norms. Such an approach does not eliminate the tension between the moral validity of law and the social facticity of that same law. In practice, Habermas demonstrates that the dichotomy of natural law and legal positivism cannot be resolved because the tension between facticity and legitimacy of law is constitutive to modern democracy.

## DEMOCRACY AND LAW

In one particular aspect, Habermas's position on law and morality resembles that of Hart and Raz: his argument that the positivity of modern law is its most important feature and that legal validity cannot be assessed by the criterion of its compatibility with natural morality. There is no substantial moral law that transcends positive legislation. At the same time, Habermas does not reject the importance of moral scrutiny of law, and he agrees in practice with Hart and Raz that such scrutiny is a constitutive element of democratic politics in modernity.

The most important difference and, for me, main advantage of Habermas's position compared with those of Hart and Raz is his radicalization of the democratic dimension of law, morality, and politics. In Hart, the moral justification of legal norms is a critical and rational enterprise that is executed in a utilitarian fashion. A philosopher can make such a critique by paying attention to the factual preferences of individuals. In the end, these preferences constitute legitimate ground for legal rights and duties (which have moral connotations).

Democracy as envisioned by Hart is thus mostly a way to legitimately regulate the relationship between state and individual. Raz seeks to overcome Hart's individualism and offers a perfectionistic version of liberalism that comprises the duty on behalf of the state to secure opportunities for meaningful personal choices, for instance, in practice, to secure the plurality of social communities in a liberal democracy.

Although Raz is right when he questions the reductionism of the individualistic interpretation of personal freedom in Hart's liberalism, his own theory includes a problematic weakening of the potential of a political-moral critique of law. While Hart believes that a moral critique of law on behalf of citizens and philosophers is crucial to progressive politics, Raz argues that only the constitutions of totalitarian regimes are morally illegitimate. On the one hand, he agrees with Hart that *individuals* do not have *moral* duty to obey legally valid norms unless those laws are justified morally. On the other hand, Raz does not regard the moral justification of law as an important democratic practice. So long as communities and meaningful alternatives for personal life are preserved, the moral scrutiny of law becomes a matter of personal morality rather than a political project.

Habermas's theory of law and democracy connects a moral critique of law with politics far more productively than Hart's and Raz's. Both morality and law are immanent to social practices, Habermas argues. Those practices in modern democracies are essentially discursive, but this discursiveness is seriously challenged and disturbed by capitalist markets and contemporary forms of mass media.[47] The moral critique of law is not a philosophical, but a political enterprise, according to Habermas. Social norms are constructed and reconstructed by means of collective practices, which implies that citizens, not philosophers, are critics of law.

As we have seen, Hart locates the critical level of morality in the rational activity of the philosopher. In order to preserve the link between this activity and democracy, Hart wants his philosopher to be utilitarian and remain skeptical of abstract moral rights. Habermas here makes a shrewd move. He agrees with Hart that fundamental rights are not natural moral rights but the products of legislation. Yet, the process of democratic will-formation includes a critical dimension that connects social facticity of rights with moral scrutiny of legal norms. Rights in a modern democracy appear in a particular legal form, and there is no moral substance of rights that can be discovered *in abstracto*: the legal form is essential for rights as socially constructed norms.

Habermas agrees with Hart that rational deliberation in normative matters is both possible and necessary as a dimension of democratic decision-making. However, Habermas's view of democracy explicitly challenges the aggregative model of democracy. In Hart, individuals' preferences and perspectives are prior to public debates. Although progressive politicians are expected to rationally argue for their positions, utilitarian political ethics still reenforces the view that what is right is an aggregation of individuals' interests. In Habermas's deliberative model, social communication is structured in such a way as to secure rational deliberation in the formal public sphere (such as for example parliamentary bodies and courts) by securing communicative power of the informal public sphere. Discussing the advantages of the republican understanding of politics Habermas writes: "A deliberative practice of self-legislation can develop only in the interplay between, on the one hand, the parliamentary will-formation institutionalized in legal procedures and programmed to reach decisions and, on the other hand, political opinion-formation along informal channels of political communication."[48] In such a deliberative model, citizens construct and re-construct their opinions rather than, as in Hart, express them. Both constitutional guarantees and "an energetic civil society" are crucial to sustain a democratic public sphere in which citizens co-construct rather than express their opinions and preferences.[49]

This means that for Habermas, democracy, practiced discursively and mediated by law, is the real source of both positivity and legitimacy. As already noted, Habermas believes that he offers a reconstruction of the self-understanding of democratic rule of law rather than a description of existing democracies. There is always a tension between, on the one hand, a self-understanding incarnated in politically active citizens, and, on the other, the factual institutions of existing democracies. Importantly, this tension is not something we can eliminate. Rather, it is the source of critique and social development.

Contrary to Raz, who views the substantive contents of non-totalitarian constitutions as the main model of legitimate legal orders, Habermas views constitutionality as a political process and therefore a source for ongoing moral scrutiny of legal norms. Constitutional principles are not an instrument for legitimizing state power, as tends to be the case in Raz, but a discursive construction and an instrument for making a differently framed critique of existing positive norms and institutions. In his discussion of human rights, Habermas describes the interweaving of moral contents of human dignity as a constitutional principle in which coercive laws are an "explosive-fusion" through "which the construction of just political orders must be performed."[50]

Habermas addresses the dialectics of normativity and positivity of modern law in a way that challenges the liberal paradigm endorsed by both Hart and Raz. There is no universally valid morality of individual rights that can secure the legitimacy of democratic legal order according to Habermas. Such legitimacy is always a political project and constitutional in the sense that democratic will-formation and political struggle are mediated by law. It is neither possible nor desirable to look for a normative theory that offers universal criteria for substantially valid norms. What a Habermasian philosopher should do is remain "constitutional" and serve democratic will-formation, which means that she must focus on the critical analysis of social processes of justification.

Thus, the substance of morally valid social norms is not to be found outside social practices mediated by language and law. What is more, social norms are justified collectively; Habermas never reduces politics to relationships between state power and the individual. Private persons become citizens—for instance, the authors of the constitution and laws—when they become involved in collective practices of justification. The philosopher should therefore focus on a critical analysis of precisely this: forms of discursive justification. She abandons her historically established identity as the main subject of social critique because this critique is now performed through social discourses.

As already stated, I interpret Habermas as a critical theorist. Critical theory seeks to uncover injustices, despite their being differently constructed, and to empower progressive political agency. Where Karl Marx believed that his political economy served the progressive course of proletarian revolution and proletarian democracy, and feminist critical theory offers instruments for political struggle against patriarchy, Habermas's project aspires to serve the project of radicalizing democracy. A characteristic feature of Habermas's critical theory is his view of personal freedom as dialectically related to political autonomy, which means that he endorses neither an abstract theory of liberal rights nor perfectionistic forms of Marxism as *the* model for social emancipation. If the political autonomy of citizens is fundamental for democratic politics, there can be no universally valid substantial aim for such a politics beyond concrete political projects to radicalize democracy.

Habermas's intention to reinterpret in a dialectic manner rather than overcome the tension between positivity and legitimacy of social norms in democracy is related to his view of social emancipation. A highly efficient tool for social critique, this dialectical approach distinguishes Habermas's theory from analytical liberal theories of, for example, Hart and Raz. Although both Hart and Raz endorse moral critique of law, they do not regard the claim to legitimacy on behalf of positive law as a politically "explosive-fusion" that democratic constitutionalism should preserve. In Hart, citizens' critique of the moral quality of positive law is crucial for democracy. However, this critique is reduced to individuals' claim to personal freedom in relation to the state. Like Hart, Raz recognizes individuals' right to question the moral legitimacy of legally valid norms. Nevertheless, on a constitutional level, he regards most existing *social orders* as fundamentally legitimate.

In my view, Habermas's dialectical interpretation of the relationship between social facticity and normative legitimacy has the potential to enable radical critiques of unjust social and legal orders. When Habermas abandons social contract theory, he distances himself from the Rawlsian project of presenting liberalism as a project of both justice and democracy. As we have seen, Habermas wants to jettison the idealism in Rawls's social contract theory. Even more importantly, Habermas does not regard justified social institutions as liberal institutions stable over time. While he endorses liberal rights in practice, he views them as particular social constructions of a political culture and not as essential components of a universally valid constitutional order.

In fairness to Rawls, it should be noted that his criterion of social stability is neither a description nor a legitimization of factual institutions. Rather, he is looking for an ideal model to justify a rational critique of social arrangements.[51] However, the ideal of a stable well-ordered society in Rawls is free from any justified skepticism of liberal versions of human rights. Those rights, not democratic politics, form the essential components of a constitutional order upon which rational and reasonable people can agree. In Rawls, society is either liberal-democratic or unjust.

To sum up the discussion so far, the main advantage of Habermas's understanding of the relationship between positivity and legitimacy of law is its dialectical character. It is neither possible nor desirable to transcend the tension between the claim to moral legitimacy on behalf of modern law, and its legal form as coerciveness and positivity. Democratic politics is not the trans-moral project depicted by Carl Schmitt and some contemporary leftists. Nor has such a politics a final destination akin to Rawls's "essentials" of liberal constitutions or the classless society of historical materialism. In Habermas's theory of law, both morality and politics are understood as constructed through social practices.

As already stated, I argue in favor of a particular, for instance, critical, reading of Habermas's theory of law and democracy. On this reading, the legal form of social norms is a form of institutional political power. Due to the law's claim to legitimacy, this power is an object of moral scrutiny; due to its positivity, such scrutiny can only be conducted by means of practical discourses.

## CRITIQUE OF HABERMAS

Habermas's dialectical approach to positivity and legitimacy of the law is thus highly valuable resource for a critical analysis of contemporary societies. Let me now address the elements of Habermas's approach that weaken the critical potential of his understanding of the relationship between law, morality, and politics.

Like any theory, Habermas's theory of modern law and its relation to politics and morality includes normative assumptions that can be challenged. Most importantly, his formal (procedural) theory of moral and democratic justification of social norms is normatively egalitarian. Although Habermas distances himself from social contract theory in the Kantian tradition, he endorses its fundamental idea that moral law as the product of practical reason has an essentially egalitarian form: "With moral questions, humanity or a presupposed republic of world citizens constitutes the reference system for justifying regulations that lie in the equal interest of all. In principle, the decisive reasons must be acceptable to each and everyone."[52]

The very fact that Habermas's theory has this dogmatically egalitarian dimension does not trouble me. This is because I do not read Habermas's theory as a description of social institutions. Nor is it a theory of how people reason when they reason about practical questions. Inequality is indeed much more "factual" than equality, even in functional democracies. Nevertheless, it is the normative force of moral equality that modern law incorporates when it presents itself as a servant of freedom. While this law is not "naturally moral," its legitimacy has a moral dimension in the form of the concrete political struggles on behalf of those who experience inequality as unjust.

What troubles me as a critical theorist is thus not the assumption that moral reason is egalitarian. Rather, it is another of Habermas's assumptions: his rejection of the possibility of a radical alternative to capitalism as an economic and social system that needs to be questioned. Habermas is right when he states that democratic politics does not have a teleology. Neither liberal rights nor perfectionistic socialism can be plausibly presented as universally valid moral projects that we should strive to implement. However, if the law in modernity and post-modernity is to preserve its claim to legitimacy in a Habermasian way, the possibility of radical change must be acknowledged.

Habermas describes himself as a reformist and "the last Marxist." At the same time, he does not regard the notion of revolution as productive for the analysis of contemporary society. In his own words: "I don't think that there can be any type of revolution in societies that have such a degree of complexity; we can't go back anyway, in spite of all the romanticist anti-movements. For academics, revolution is a notion of the nineteenth century."[53]

Obviously, Habermas endorses the view of revolution as a modern phenomenon. On this account, most illuminatively systematized by John Dunn, "revolutions are a form of massive, violent and rapid social change. They are also attempts to embody a set of values in a new or at least renovated social order."[54] Most importantly, modern revolutions, that historically have imitated previous (modern) revolutions,[55] all include the belief in the possibility of "realizing all together superior form of collective life."[56] Habermas seems to agree with John Dunn when he rejects the theoretical potential of this category of revolution. He cannot envision a radical alternative to capitalism with its extraordinary social complexity which implies that revolutionary anti-movements appear as romanticist.

In his most elegant interventions in discussions of contemporary legislations of markets, such as for example, the European Monetary Union,[57] Habermas restrains from radical critique of injustices of financial capitalism. Although we know that such interventions according to Habermas himself are political rather than philosophical practice (we have learned that the philosopher as philosopher should not offer particular normative solutions), they cohere with Habermas's basic skepticism toward the concept of revolution.

I believe that Habermas is wrong when he views radical critics of capitalism as romanticists all together. Several theorists have pointed out that the fact that *we* cannot see an alternative to complex capitalist society does not support the idea that the notion of revolution is not relevant for contemporary political analysis. Revolutions tend to surprise even revolutionaries, let alone reformists, because they are explosively democratic: their subjects create their own political subjectivity even as the old order is undergoing destruction.[58]

Moreover, Habermas's conceptualization of revolution implies a return to a less complex class society. Why? Igor Shoikhedbrod argues that this view is a consequence of Habermas's "misinterpretation" of Marxian theory. Shoikhedbrod writes: "What Habermas rejects outright is a fully-fledged version of economic democracy, in which the steering function of the market (price mechanism) is eliminated and replaced by a totalizing vision of associated production."[59] However, such a totalizing vision of production is hardly a necessary element of anti-capitalist movements. Neither is it a defining feature of Marxian theory of revolution.

I think that an additional, and possibly the most plausible, explanation of Habermas's understanding of anti-capitalism as romanticism is his unwillingness to imagine a global world from any other point of view than that of Western modernity. If social revolution is a matter of radical social transformation, as I believe it is, revolutionary agency in today's globalized world need not be linked to the public spheres of countries like Germany and the United States. Habermas may be right that many contemporary Western anti-capitalist movements are romanticist,[60] but this does not mean that all movements are. This is especially true if we theorize capitalism as a global rather than an entirely modern phenomenon.

Let us turn to the issue of law, politics, and morality in order to illustrate this point. Although Habermas is aware of the importance of law for capitalist markets, he does not consider these kinds of legal regulations as fundamentally *constitutional*. We can, of course, read such a possibility into his scheme of rights, but, as we have seen, social and economic rights in Habermas's scheme function as a relatively harmless complement to political rights. In a global perspective, I claim, the legislation on economic relations has constitutional importance because it is crucial to the very possibility of democratic sovereignty of many societies. Even functional liberal democracies with advanced economies such as Sweden are subject to the external legal regulations of capital, rather than being the authors of such regulations.

I think that Habermas's theory of democracy—its law and morality—will improve if it incorporates the view that the legislating of basic economic relationships should be a matter of democratic constitutionalism. This implies the possibility of revolutionary changes.

The global structures of capital in the current stage of capitalism are mediated by law. Moreover, they are mediated by the positive law of the most powerful countries, mainly the United States.[61] Does this kind of law include the claim to legitimacy in Habermasian terms? I doubt it. Rather, the very fact of such mediation is effectively removed from political agendas of contemporary democracies. If I am right, the critique of law becomes moral and radically democratic when it dares to address the legal code of capital. If, on the other hand, the existing legal regulations of capital do not aspire for democratic legitimacy (and I believe they do not) there is clearly space for a democratic revolution in the system of wealth production.

Back in 1982, Johannes Berger criticized Habermas for lacking the tools to address the most fundamental tensions within contemporary capitalism. In his "Die Versprachlichung des Sakralen und die Entsprachlichung der Ökonomie," Berger argued that Habermas's theory of communicative action, as opposed to strategic aim-oriented action, underestimates the social importance of conflicts immanent in systems such as economics and the state. At that point in time, Habermas believed that the main conflict in the current stage of capitalism disclosed by his analysis was the system-rationality colonizing lifeworld thus suppressing the communicative rationality immanent in that lifeworld. Berger objected that systems such as economics are marked by internal conflicts that are not reducible to the colonization of the lifeworld by the strategic rationality of formally organized systems. Moreover, there are important tensions between systems—economics and government, for example—that Habermas's language-philosophy and sociology overlook.[62]

In his later writings, Habermas developed his theory of modern democracy, in many regards moving beyond the theory of communicative action. The Habermas of *Between Facts and Norms* is not a philosopher of language bent on expanding the analysis of communication to the realm of sociology. Nonetheless, his approach to the facticity and normativity of modern law does not include an analysis of the legally framed relationship between the economic system of current capitalism and democracy.

Habermas's approach to the dialectics of positivity and legitimacy of modern law is elegant and politically potent. It would become even more potent if its analysis of the positivity and legitimacy of the law were extended to include legal mediations of the most important source of power, namely capital. In this particular regard, I disagree with those who argue that the analysis of law in *Between Facts and Norms*, in order to be critical, must be complemented by "critique of political economy" in a more traditional Marxian way.[63] Rather, the potential of Habermas's critique of the relationship between legality and facticity should be expanded to the constitutionality of legal regulations of economy.

Is it possible, then, to expand the Habermasian view of democratic constitutionalism to incorporate an analysis of the legal regulations of economic relationships and wealth production?

In my view, such an extension presupposes that a theory of law and democracy incorporates an analysis of global economic structures and political agencies beyond the self-understanding of Western *modernity*. Not only the political importance of legally regulating global economic agencies but the experiences of colonialism and post-colonialism of many contemporary societies should be highlighted. These experiences reveal injustices that are invisible from the viewpoint of Western modernity.

In what follows, I modify Habermas's theory of law, morality, and politics in two directions. First, I further radicalize his ethical and social constructivism. Second, I argue that a reasonable defense of modernity as a political and social project should be methodologically restricted to what Habermas views as a self-understanding of Western democratic constitutionalism. Such a reduction is compatible with a critical theory of modern law only if it explicitly counteracts the risk of holding up Western political projects as *the* normative model for democracy.

## NOTES

1. Habermas, *Between Facts and Norms*, 447.
2. Jürgen Habermas, *Autonomy and Solidarity* (London: Verso, 1986), 160.
3. See, for example, Hugh Baxter, *Habermas: The Discourse Theory of Law and Democracy* (Redwood City, CA: Stanford University Press, 2011). Baxter expects

Habermas's principles of justification to be "directly applicable" to democratic legislation and adjudication (chapters 2 and 3). See also, Daniel Gaus, "Rational Reconstruction as a Method of Political Theory between Social Critique and Empirical Political Science." *Constellations* 20, no. 4 (2013): 553–570.

4. Habermas, *Between Facts and Norms*, 447.

5. Ibid., 445–446.

6. Jürgen Habermas, "Fundamentalism and Terror," in *Philosophy in a Time of Terror. Dialogues with Jürgen Habermas and Jacques Derrida,* ed. Giovanna Borradori (Chicago: The University of Chicago Press, 2003), 38.

7. Habermas, *Between Facts and Norms*, 176.

8. Ibid., 129–130.

9. In another context, Habermas claims fundamental rights to be "the recognized foundation of constitutionality." Jürgen Habermas, "Natural Law and Revolution," in Jürgen Habermas, *Theory and Practice* (London: Heinemann Educational Books, 1974), 113.

10. Habermas, "Natural Law and Revolution," 111.

11. Igor Shoikhedbrod, "Revolution or legality? Confronting the specter of Marx in Habermas's legal philosophy," *Contemporary Political Theory* 20, no. 1 (2020): 72–95.

12. Habermas, "Natural Law and Revolution," 115.

13. Habermas, *Between Facts and Norms*, 82.

14. Habermas, "Natural Law and Revolution," 96.

15. Habermas, *Between Facts and Norms*, 122.

16. Jürgen Habermas, *Moral Consciousness and Communicative Action* (Cambridge, UK: Polity Press, 1990), 66.

17. Jürgen Habermas, *Justification and Application* (Cambridge, UK: Polity Press, 1993), 89.

18. Habermas, *Between Facts and Norms*, 122.

19. Ibid., 123.

20. Habermas is critical of the liberal view of human rights because it reduces their function to "only *limiting* effect." For Habermas, it is not enough that rights limit power of the state—fundamental rights should "become effective for offering [. . .] positive guarantees for participation." Habermas, "Natural Law and Revolution," 115.

21. Habermas, *Between Facts and Norms*, 128.

22. Habermas, *Moral Consciousness and Communicative Action*, 68.

23. Ibid., 66.

24. Ibid., 65.

25. Habermas, *Between Facts and Norms*, 110.

26. Ibid., 110.

27. Ibid., 453.

28. Ibid., 56–63.

29. Ibid., 9.

30. Ibid., 106–107.

31. Ibid., 110.

32. Jürgen Habermas, "Human Dignity and the Realistic Utopia of Human Rights," *Metaphilosophy* 41, no. 4 (2010): 471.

33. Habermas, *Between Facts and Norms*, 110.

34. Ibid., 156–157.

35. Habermas, "Human Dignity and the Realistic Utopia of Human Rights," *Metaphilosophy* 41, no. 4 (2010): 464–480.

36. Ibid., 467.

37. Ibid., 469.

38. Ibid., 476.

39. Rainer Forst, *Justification and Critique* (Cambridge, UK: Polity, 2014), 54–56.

40. Habermas, *Between Facts and Norms*, 204.

41. Ronald Dworkin, *Justice in Robes* (Cambridge, MA: Harvard University Press, 2006), 35.

42. Ibid., 4.

43. Dworkin's view of political morality is in practice Rawlsian and thus vulnerable to a critique that is directed to Rawls's view of "the constitutional essentials" as moral principles all political liberals agree about.

44. On the asymmetry between claims to propositional truth and claims to normative rightness, see, for example, Habermas, *Moral Consciousness and Communicative Action*, 59–62.

45. Habermas, *Between Facts and Norms*, 201–203.

46. Ibid., 3.

47. To properly interpret Habermas's theory of modern law demands to see its background in the discourse theory. For a nuanced analysis and critique of the relationship between discourse theory and theory of law in Habermas, see, for example, Mikael Spång, *Emancipation, Democracy and Modern Critique of Law. Reconsidering Habermas* (London: Palgrave Macmillan, 2018).

48. Habermas, *Between Facts and Norms*, 275.

49. Ibid., 369.

50. Habermas, "Human Dignity and the Realistic Utopia of Human Rights," 479.

51. John Rawls, *Political Liberalism.* Expanded edition (New York: Columbia University Press, 1993), 35–47.

52. Habermas, *Between Facts and Norms*, 108.

53. Jürgen Habermas, "Concluding Remarks," in *Habermas and the Public Sphere*, ed. Craig Calhoun (Cambridge, MA: The MIT Press, 1992), 469.

54. John Dunn, *Modern Revolutions. An Introduction to the Analysis of a Political Phenomenon.* Second edition (Cambridge, UK: Cambridge University Press, 1994), 11.

55. Dunn, *Modern Revolutions*, 232.

56. John Dunn, "Revolution as a Political Category'," in: *Future(s) of the Revolution and the Reformation*, ed. Elena Namli (London: Palgrave Macmillan, 2019), 32.

57. Jürgen Habermas, *The Lure of Technocracy* (Cambridge, UK: Polity, 2015).

58. Boris Kapustin, "What May Be Wrong with the 'End' in the End-of-Revolution Thesis?" in *Future(s) of the Revolution and the Reformation*, 121–152.

59. Shoikhedbrod, "Revolution or legality? Confronting the spectre of Marx in Habermas's legal philosophy," 89.

60. For an alternative interpretation of radical agency, see Håkan Thörn, "Revolution as a politics of time-space. From enlightenment modernity to advanced globality," in *Future(s) of the Revolution and the Reformation*, 65–96.

61. Katharina Pistor, *The Code of Capital. How the Law Creates Wealth and Inequality* (Princeton, NJ: Princeton University Press, 2019), 1–22.

62. Johannes Berger, "Die Versprachlichung des Sakralen und die Entsprachlichung der Ökonomie," *Zeitschrift für Soziologie* 11, heft 4 (1982): 353–365.

63. William E. Scheuermann, "Capitalism, Law, and Social Criticism," *Constellations* 20, no. 4 (2013): 571–586.

# Chapter 6

# Legal Positivism, Democracy, and Moral Critique of Law

As I noted in the introduction, my aim in this volume is to frame legal positivism as a theory of the relationship between law and morality, a theory offering critical resources of democratic and moral nature. In order to realize such an ambition, we need to free our analysis of modern law from both the Platonism of natural law and the political cynicism incorporated in many forms of legal positivism. While the Platonism of the natural law tradition—the term used by Habermas and discussed in previous chapters—is an idealistic paradigm that can be framed in various ways, it essentially regards some ideational forms as pre-given models for actual normative orders to "copy." In most cases, particular understandings of human nature and reason are presented as pre-given *ideas*, to be taken as fundamental when contextual normative orders are evaluated and reshaped. Although such ideas need not be static or include advanced metaphysics, they are viewed as primary with regard to social practices. One of the most familiar examples of such an idealism is the traditional Western view of human rights. Different approaches—secular as well as Christian—are most often united by the idea that there exists a universal moral ground for international human rights law and that this ground cannot be reasonably questioned.

Interestingly, even classical legal positivism such as that of Hans Kelsen states that morality, in order to have relevance for positive legislation, should be absolute and pre-given. This assumption, or, rather, the fact that scholars cannot discover such a morality, is one of the most important reasons behind Kelsen's skepticism toward the natural law tradition. However, other forms of legal positivism are disconnected from this naturalistic understanding of morality and instead see both moral and legal regulations as the products of social practices. Political cynicism enters the scene when theorists argue that moral considerations have no relevance at all for political actions, above all legislation.

The model of legal positivism that I have been pursuing in this investigation rejects the idealism of the natural law and regards moral and legal regulations as social practices. However, a materialistic understanding of morality and law need not lead to the rejection of a critical level of morality. Critical morality plays an important role when legal orders are scrutinized, developed, and replaced by new orders. Thus, our aim should be to preserve materialistic insights into the sociality of law and, simultaneously, demonstrate how morality helps democratic agents to remain critical in relation to positive law in their society.

What can we say about this enterprise after our analysis of Hart's, Raz's, and Habermas's theories of law, morality, and politics? As we have seen, these three models, though elegant and theoretically potent, are nowhere critical to the degree that can reasonably be expected from a progressive theory of law, politics, and morality. Yet, I believe that it is possible to use Hart, Raz, and Habermas as resources for strengthening legal positivism as a critical theory. In what follows, I argue in favor of a theory of law that reconciles the separation thesis with a non-positivistic epistemology of law, above all, while including a constructivist account of both conventional and critical morality. Additionally, I will demonstrate that deontological ethics offers greater critical potential with relation to social regulations than both virtue ethics and utilitarianism.

Thus, a tenable model of legal positivism reaffirms the separation thesis: legal validity does not necessarily include moral criteria. Most importantly, it is always the case that there are legally valid norms which fail the test of moral justification. Even when the legislator incorporates elements of moral justification into the test of legal validity (by means of constitutional principles, for example), legally valid norms are still a result of an exercise of power and appear differently (i.e., as just or unjust) to different social groups. This is mostly a consequence of unequal access to economic, social, and discursive power. In some cases, even cultural differences influence the experience of social institutions as just or unjust.

The different forms of racism normalized in modern Western democracies are one telling example. While European anti-discrimination law appears just or even morally radical from majoritarian perspectives, many European minorities experience the law and its implementation as far too weak an instrument for combatting discrimination and racism.[1] Most of the fundamental social structures that sustain racism are still invisible in the legal domain.[2]

Another example is how economic relations are legally framed. As critics of contemporary capitalism have demonstrated, legal regulations of wealth-production that give the wealthy global minority access to a disproportionally large amount of economic, social, and discursive power are fundamentally unjust. One dimension of this injustice is the very invisibility of "the law of capital." The global market presents itself as something beyond the political, or even as something pre-political, a condition for the very emergence of democratic politics; and the law plays a crucial ideological role in this particular manifestation.[3]

It is beyond the scope of the present investigation to develop further a critique of unjust legal regulations of economic relations. My point is that the law, which evidently creates wealth on behalf of a few, *must* hide itself from the very attention of people who are disadvantaged within social structures sustained by this law. Whenever democratic attention focuses on the legal regulation of basic economic structures, an opportunity for radical changes presents itself, thereby threatening the privileged minority.

Recognizing the existence of legally valid norms that fail moral justification or even escape its very possibility does not leave us confronting political cynicism as the sole alternative to the natural law tradition. Contrary to the claim of political cynicism that moral considerations are irrelevant for political actions, unjust and legally valid norms motivate moral critique that has a significant democratic potential. The political subjectivity of those who, because of their social position in a concrete society, see legally valid norms as morally unjustified is fundamentally related to this appearance. The very experience of social institutions as unjust is a crucial element of democratic political agency and places the critical ethicist on the side of the unprivileged.

This particular insight into the democratic potential of the separation thesis was crucial to Hart's novel version of legal positivism, and even now it makes legal positivism highly attractive for the democrat. As we have seen, Hart viewed material interests and the positions of individuals as a democratic recourse. In my view, social groups rather than individuals offer the most solid basis for political action aimed at reforming social institutions, including the law.[4]

How then should we develop legal positivism if we want to strengthen the progressive democratic potential of the separation thesis? As we have seen, there is always a risk that endorsement of legal positivism implies skepticism toward discussing social injustice and the abuse of humans, animals, and nature as normalized by the law. This risk must be acknowledged, and for this very reason the model that I defend in what follows preserves yet another crucial element of the Hartian type of legal positivism, namely a combination of the separation thesis with a non-positivistic epistemology of law.

This non-positivistic epistemology regards reasoning about law as a practical enterprise—that is, as reasoning about how to act. In that it differs from the older forms of legal positivism that incorporate positivist epistemology and regards the very theory of law as a descriptive and disengaged enterprise.

As we have seen, the "moralist" Hart defends the separation thesis while simultaneously claiming that law can only be understood from the participant's perspective. Law appears as law only for those who have to treat posited legal regulations as authoritative reasons for their agency.[5] Therefore, the scholar of law should seek to understand the law from a practical point of view. Such a perspective does not exclude normative analysis although it recognizes differences in normative reasoning applied to legal, moral, and political domains.

Dissatisfied with the older forms of legal positivism, many theorists of law incorporated this Hartian insight into their analysis. Theorists differ as to which participatory position is most relevant for understanding the law. Ronald Dworkin defends the centrality of the judge's position, while Robert Alexy sees both judges and advocates as central to the proper legal epistemology.[6] Whatever the case, nothing prevents us from expending a non-positivistic epistemology to include other practical positions within the legal domain, most importantly, to citizens as the subjects of legal regulations.[7]

The critical legal positivism being defended here thus allows theorists of law to endorse the separation thesis without endorsing a positivistic epistemology that reduces studies of law to a descriptive enterprise performed by a disengaged observer. Critical legal positivism invites scholars of law to serve the reformer, to become instrumental for those who find positive law unjust, and to make this insight into an issue for democratic struggle and institutional reform.

## CLAIM TO LEGITIMACY: FROM METAPHYSICS TO A DEMOCRATIC DISCOURSE

The separation thesis, if combined with a non-positivistic epistemology of law, is the most important feature of legal positivism, which, I am arguing, is critical in nature and therefore socially progressive. Furthermore, this positivism does not view sanctions and direct coercion on behalf of the state power as the most fundamental sociological element of law. As Hart and Raz argue, the stable functioning of legal rules, though related to sanctions and coercion, is fundamentally dependent upon the non-coercive social compliance of citizens and authorities.

For both Hart and Raz, the argument in support of this understanding of law is the fact that law (even the most unjust law we know of) claims that its authority is morally justified and therefore reasonably deserving of compliance. Hart recognizes that there exist in societies disadvantaged groups for which the legal system cannot be presented as just. Those groups, he claims, have no reason to comply with legal rules other than the threat of sanctions.

However, citizens with reasonable access to political power and/or social resources expect the law's authority to be justified, not merely enforced by the threat of sanctions.

In my view, Hartian approach to law as deserving non-coercive compliance adds an important element to critique of ideology as legitimization of power. In order to keep legal systems functional, privileged groups invest in different projects of ideology production and thereby seek to present legal regulations of social relationships as legitimate.[8] Therefore, scrutiny of moral quality of valid legal rules can contribute to critique of fundamental social structures.

The claim to justified authority on behalf of the law makes the moral critique of legal regulations a meaningful democratic enterprise. As subjects of law, we are all bound by the authority of law, for instance, we have to comply with its demands even when we regard them as wrong or unjust. At the same time, as democratic agents, we can and should utilize our dissatisfaction with the moral quality of legal rules in order to change them by means of various political processes.

Most importantly, the type of legal positivism which Hart introduces places responsibility for the moral quality of the legal system on citizens rather than lawyers. This is so because there is no "natural morality" that can secure morally justified interpretation of the law by the professional lawyer (such as Dworkin's justice Hercules). The moral critique of law, which Hartian legal positivism encourages, is social in nature and related to positions occupied by unprivileged individuals and groups in different societies. Moreover, a critical theorist like myself believes that most lawyers have little, if any, personal experience of social injustice, something that makes them even less inclined to approach social institutions critically.[9]

In critical legal positivism, a social constructivist understanding of morality replaces the moral realism of natural law. Such a move makes it possible to question the law's claim to legitimacy without turning to natural morality as the main critical resource. Conventional morality is obviously a social construction, that is, a dimension of social relationships. Even more importantly, critical morality is a product of social relationships rather than a result of philosophical or theological insights about human nature, reason, and so on. Conventional moral norms and values seem justified to those who benefit from the moral regulations (which may or may not be incorporated into the law) within a particular society, while the disadvantaged have material reasons for scrutinizing the legitimacy of conventional morality. The ethicist can and should assist this kind of critical enterprise on behalf of those who question the legitimacy of moral conventions.[10]

It is of course possible, and in many cases efficient, to use the belief in human nature as worthy of being dignified in order to demonstrate that particular legal rules or entire legal systems are unjust. A famous example is the resistance strategy adopted by the civil rights movement in the United States. But even this particular example demonstrates that experiences of racism and lack of power, rather than ideological or religious insights about universal human nature, are what drive people to question the moral quality of positive law.

Additionally, a constructivist perspective on the moral critique of law implies that any sufficient improvement of moral quality of legal regulations is a political enterprise. Raz is right in stating that the critique of law can only be critique of social relations protected by this law. An unjust law is one whose authority is an instrument for the preservation of social relations marked by injustices such as inequality or domination. However, there is no natural morality that can expose social injustices in such a way that different social agents will agree about "obviously" morally progressive reforms. Whether one conceives of existing social institutions as just or unjust depends on one's social position. To change unjust institutions is a matter of political struggle and hence access to power.

A constructivist who admits that critical morality is a result of material positions that make particular social relations appear as unjust, need not embrace political cynicism. Experiences of the unprivileged make social structures appear as unjust and access to power is crucial in order to change such structures. Yet, *moral* critique of social injustice has the potential to bring about political subjectivity in a progressive, albeit never completely morally justified, form. Democratic agents who frame their dissatisfaction with social structures as a question of moral justice face the challenge of justifying their critique of established normative orders as well as their programs for reform to other—ideally all—social groups in society. Thus, when a critical ethicist elaborates on normative ethics and ethical theory, she should aim to serve progressive social agency, strengthen its self-reflexivity and its will to critical deliberation.

It is here that different models of democratic politics enter the scene. In our case, Hart, Raz, and Habermas obviously differ in their respective view of democracy. Although Hart admits the existence of unprivileged social groups that lack any incitement to comply with the law other than fear of sanctions, he does not regard underprivileged social groups as crucial agents of democratic politics. A committed liberal democrat, Hart tends to reduce political agency to individual agency and depicts democratic politics in terms of relationships between individual citizens and the state. The reformer, whom Hart's legal positivism was designed to serve, seeks to protect individual freedoms and secure justice as a dimension of the relationship between state and individual.

In my view, this precisely explains why Hart in the end rejects the theory of moral rights as a form of critical ethics. He conceives of deontological ethics from the perspective of the state as duty-holder and is therefore rightly skeptical of the idea of natural rights being protected by such duties. What Hart overlooks is a possibility to offer a normative theory of rights based on the subjectivity of underprivileged groups who demand recognition of legitimacy of their *claims*. Such a theory need not incorporate the metaphysical foundationalism of natural law theory. A constructivist theory of rights does not view legally protected rights as a kind of natural morality of duties (on behalf of the state) that is implemented through positive law. Nor does it imply that the human dignity of all individuals simply "exists," awaiting discovering by the uncorrupted practical reason of philosophers.

A constructivist theory of rights such as that found in Habermas's political theory views both human rights and the constitutional principle of respect for human dignity as a result of social practices. In contrast to Hart, who believes that the ideal of protecting human dignity can be easily turned into paternalistic and anti-democratic state politics, Habermas understands legally protected rights as concrete social demands acknowledged by means of a democratic legislation that is in turn a political process. Such a politics is an arena for communicative rationality as well as for pragmatic dealing with social conflicts. For this reason, social groups and movements capable of organized agency are the most important political subjects of any progressive social or legal reform.

In the legal positivism I am here defending, the law's claim to moral legitimacy is thus disconnected from the metaphysical heritage of the natural law tradition. This claim has an important social function, namely, to *present* legal regulations as morally justified and therefore as warranting non-coercive compliance by all citizens. The legitimizing of law as something coherent with justified morality is an element of ideology production, which also means that disconnecting legal validity from moral legitimacy makes ideologies of power both explicit and possible to critique.

Simultaneously, when made on behalf of the law, the same claim makes moral critique—both of the law and the ideologies which present valid law as justified—a politically progressive activity. The social experiences of concrete forms of injustice which are codified by law become a democratic recourse precisely because the law claims to be morally legitimate.

## LEGISLATION AS THE CRUCIAL PRACTICE OF POLITICAL MORALITY

Legal positivism as a theory of law and morality does not reject the social importance of the moral quality of legal rules. This importance is political in nature because the moral critique of posited legal norms is a democratic rather than theoretical enterprise. Political agents question the moral quality of the law in order to reform society by means of new legal regulations. Such an understanding of the moral quality of law leads naturally to the view that legislation is the main arena for the moral critique of law.

This does not mean that explicit moral reasoning cannot become an element of the legal practice in *sensu stricto*. As we have already seen, Hart recognizes the possibility of incorporating moral principles into legal systems. When this is done, constitutional courts can be viewed as arenas for scrutinizing the moral quality of positive regulations. However, if we endorse ethical constructivism—and I believe we should—constitutional courts using moral principles in order to assess the moral quality of legislation become political to the extent they in fact perform such a task. This is illustrated most clearly in the political history of the United States. Moral principles incorporated in the United States Constitution are interpreted and applied differently by judges in accordance with their own political preferences.[11]

As I have argued elsewhere,[12] moral principles such as the principle of equal respect for human dignity should be utilized in adjudicating human rights cases. Crucially, an egalitarian interpretation of human dignity allows lawyers to counteract discrimination in cases where different rights come into conflict. However, we should never expect that such a usage would by itself secure the moral quality of the law.

Some critics of legal positivism, such as Dworkin, believe that adjudication based on fundamental moral principles should perform the task of securing the moral quality of the law. They argue that there is a particular moral dimension in the law that can be actualized in adjudication in order to reach "true" legal judgments.[13] This position is deficient if evaluated from the perspective of social constructivism because it presupposes the existence of objective moral principles that are necessarily reached by coherent moral reasoning (of the judge). According to the kind of constructivism that I defend, the meaning (as well as the lack of meaning) of moral principles, while not created by individual judges, is dependent on contextual factors.

Thus, "moral adjudication" cannot guarantee moral quality of law because there is no such thing as *the* morally correct adjudication. There are, of course, cases where it is possible for the legal profession to reach a broad moral consensus, but most urgent cases of injustice appear as moral dilemmas. For those who invest their resources in producing new medicine, the firm legal protection of property rights seems morally just. For those who cannot afford medicine distributed by capitalist markets, it is highly reasonable that property rights should be limited and some kind of re-distribution is justified.

This and similar moral dilemmas cannot be resolved by morally informed reasoning on the part of judges. Although some judges would like to believe that their interpretation of law is morally true, in practice they exercise practical reason from particular perspectives that can and should be challenged.

As already noted, I do not reject the legitimacy of moral reasoning in the legal domain. Transparent moral reasoning in hard cases is more democratic than usage of judicial discretion. This is because only transparently presented reasoning can be challenged by alternative reasoning. However, if the judge claims that she offers a morally true interpretation of the law, her moral reasoning in practice becomes a form of judicial discretion—professional monopoly on the moral knowledge. The more political judicial review becomes, the more important it is to question the belief in the existence of morally true adjudication.

This implies, for example, that Dworkin's interpretative theory of adjudication makes much more sense if we abandon his cognitivism. It remains possible to argue that the egalitarian principle of equal respect and concern should guide legal reasoning in hard cases. If interpreted within the paradigm of social constructivism, however, the principle does not risk being depoliticized because its meaning and application are open to competing perspectives.

In my view, there is nothing in Hart, Raz, or Habermas that prevents us from acknowledging some political potential of "moral" adjudication in hard cases. However, this potential is limited due to several reasons. First and most important is the fact that unjust legal regulations can seem uncontroversial to lawyers and do not qualify for hard cases. Fundamental forms of social injustices that have been codified by law are seldom objects of judicial disagreements. Gender inequality, colonialism, and racism are among the social relationships that have been, and in many cases remain, codified by positive law without causing any disagreement among lawyers[14] about how the law should be interpreted.

A second reason for the limited democratic potential of moral adjudication is the sociological dimension of adjudication that was mentioned earlier. As several proponents of critical legal studies have demonstrated, adjudication is a practice influenced by the social position of the judge as well as by her ideological preferences.[15]

There is, of course, nothing unexpected about such findings for those who endorse a constructivist view of morality. The ideological dimension of adjudication, a constructivist claims, cannot be eliminated. At the same time, legal judgments are final in a way that neither political nor moral judgments are. This combination—legal closure *and* ideological component—explains why even legal practices that include moral aspirations have a very limited potential as an arena for political morality.

If, instead of focusing on adjudication as the arena for scrutinizing the moral quality of law, we view democratic politics as such an arena, any kind of legal regulation becomes potentially open for a critique that is also explicitly socially positioned. The particular forms of the European parliamentary democracies endorsed by Hart, Raz, and Habermas naturally influence their understandings of the proper arena for moral scrutiny of the law as that of public debate and deliberation. However, for a constructivist and a democrat these understandings seem politically potent, regardless of their particular European genealogy.

Democratic politics in its different forms—already known as well as innovative—is the proper arena for scrutinizing the moral quality of law because it has the potential to include alternative perspectives on justice that the legal domain never has. From parliamentary inquiries and various types of established political organizations to different forms of political protest, democratic politics create channels to question the legitimacy of social regulations. As already stated, the fact that such a critique is the result of experiences and material positions does not undermine the meaningfulness of moral arguments for or against particular social structures.

When a group is subjected to racism or sexism, its members have a material interest in defeating the particular social structures that cause exploitation and domination. However, such an interest in itself may or may not lead to resistance to racism and sexism. Even people subjected to exploitation and domination in most cases accept the dominant ideologies that present injustices as part of an order that cannot be changed. Moral arguments are of critical importance here because they might transform politics from the domain of the factual (to be adjusted to) into a domain of different futures (to be created). While a society without racism may sound like a utopian project, condemning racism as morally wrong and acting against racist structures is a progressive and meaningful political project.

Legal positivism as a critical theory of law and morality is thus a position that correlates with political realism on the descriptive level. Material interests, not ideational commitments, lie behind the political subjectivity of individuals, groups, and states. At the same time, my interpretation of the Hartian legal positivism treats the moral critique of social relationships and hence of legal regulations as a potent element of social life. This is so because humans, though bound by their particular social positions, are capable of imagining and longing for a different life. Justice and solidarity are not less attractive than material prosperity in the context of social and political struggle.[16]

There is no "true morality" that we can discover or agree upon regardless of social position, time, or place. Peace, justice, and freedom, like other fundamental moral categories, have different content, and our moral disagreements about that content cannot be resolved by means of a theory of morality. However, this does not mean that we cannot argue in favor of normative theories that we believe contribute to progressive social developments. I think that the principle of equal respect for humanity in each and every person is the most potent instrument for uncovering and resisting *different* forms of injustices. This principle is not a moral truth; there is no natural law to which a true formulation of the principle might correspond. Nor is it possible to prove that this principle is true and that utilitarian morality is false. But there are strong reasons to claim that the principle of equal respect for humanity is justified. Therefore, the demand for social equality as expressed through the principle of equal respect for each and everyone's humanity is a powerful critical resource within democratic politics.

Before I develop my interpretation of the principle of equal respect for human dignity further, more must be said about the different understandings of politics within the form of critical legal positivism defended here.

## MORAL CRITIQUE OF LAW: POLITICS AND REVOLUTION

Legal positivism has a critical potential precisely because it rejects any necessary connection between the legal validity of social regulations and the moral quality of those regulations. In order to expose unjust laws, we need to acknowledge the very possibility of such a thing as unjust legally valid regulations. Although legal positivism, understood as a theory of law and morality, cannot be combined with naturalistic ethics, it can, as I have argued, easily incorporate a constructivist approach to morality. Both conventional and critical morality are products of social relationships, which means that there is no universal moral law which human reason discovers in some objective manner. What do exist are the different practical positions of persons and groups, positions from which we judge and act—create, co-create, and re-create our societies.

Morality is thus a crucial dimension of social agency. Different views of justice, peace, equality, and the other fundamental moral concepts are instruments of both social struggle and social cooperation. Moral critique of law is thus basically a critique of social relationships protected by the law.

In order to further strengthen the critical potential of legal positivism that incorporates a constructivist approach to morality, the possibility of radical political agency and therefore of social revolution must be recognized. In my view, the critical and therefore democratic potential of legal positivism of Hart and Raz is weakened by their fear of revolutionary anarchy, while Habermas gives up on revolution because he believes that complexity of contemporary capitalism makes radical changes of social structures impossible.

Both Hart and Raz mistakenly identify social revolutions with episodes of institutional anarchy marked by the absence of rule of law. It is of course true that the very notion of revolution implies the risk of anarchy because revolution is defined by the possibility of creating a radically new social order. However, institutional anarchy can be part of non-revolutionary processes,[17] while revolutionary changes do not presuppose longer episodes of institutional anarchy. It is perfectly reasonable to envision radical and progressive social transformations that do not imply institutional anarchy.

There is a further component in Raz's theory that does not allow for a radical critique of injustice. As my analysis of Raz's view of morality shows, he offers a defense of perfectionistic liberalism framed in terms of an Aristotelian morality of personal development. Individual freedom is the fundamental moral value to be protected, and this freedom, according to Raz, presupposes the existence of meaningful socially pre-given alternatives for personal choices. My main objections to such a view of human freedom are that meaningful personal projects can coexist with unjust social relations and, most importantly, that their existence is not conditioned by the endorsement of social equality. Although Raz's ethics is not essentialist to the same degree as Aristotle's ethics, it preserves the conservative character of Aristotle's ethics, which in turn weakens the critical potential of Raz's legal positivism.

If I am right, Hart's and Raz's skepticism toward the radical demand for social justice and hence toward social revolution is what prevents them from applying the critical resources of legal positivism to the legal regulations of basic social structures. Hart tends to reduce the issue of moral justice to the relationship between individual and state. Raz emphasizes the importance of different communities within a state that seeks to secure the possibility of meaningful personal choices. Neither Hart nor Raz understands social justice in structural terms, which prevents them from interpreting social revolution as a radical change of social structures rather than merely an episode of revolt and anarchy.

Unlike Hart and Raz, Habermas realizes the importance of social regulations beyond the direct relationship between individuals and the state. By doing so he radicalizes the democratic resources of his theory of law, making it relevant for the critique of contemporary forms of democratic deficit. Most importantly, Habermas demonstrates how the contemporary form of capitalism has transformed the public sphere of modern democracies: it has efficiently depoliticized social issues and to a large degree pacified collective political agency.

As a critic of current developments in capitalism, Habermas continues to dismiss the possibility of a radical alternative to it. In my view, Habermas is wrong in this regard. His analysis of capitalism is deficient because it is reduced to a scrutiny of the democratic potential of Western European and North American societies. As we have seen, Habermas makes an important and highly intentional reduction in his theory of law and politics when he focuses on Western modernity. There is a huge amount of literature on the issue of Habermas's defense of modernity and I am not going to discuss it here. What is important for our purposes, however, is that Habermas's analysis and defense of European modernity has come to include the view that modern types of democracy—imperfect as they are in both Europe and the United States—are the most we can hope for. Capitalism sets and will continue to set conditions for democratic institutions. On the one hand, Habermas offers a theory of participatory democracy. On the other hand, such a democracy does not include the possibility of a radical restructuring of economic relationships.

As noted earlier, Habermas believes that contemporary capitalism does not allow for radical social transformation. However, he does not present any argument in support of the thesis that social revolution is not possible in other contexts than those of liberal democracies in the Global North. This is so simply because Habermas is ignorant of such contexts, even more ignorant than he is of religious matters, making this another sphere in which Habermas overlooks possibilities of progressive and radical democratic agency.[18]

Whether social revolutions are still possible in reality cannot be predicted by means of a theory. As many scholars of historical revolutions have pointed out, a general feature of the revolutions we know about is that they came as a surprise even to revolutionaries who had been longing and working for radical transformation.[19] In my view, it is reasonable to hope that the current unjust global order will be defeated and a new, less unjust, appear. However, no "new heaven and new earth" is ever an implementation of some theoretical or ideological schemes. Even for Karl Marx it was obvious that all a scholar of politics can hope for is the theoretical instruments that allow her to recognize and assist politically progressive social agency when it consolidates itself in and through a social struggle to improve its material and social conditions.[20]

Thus, the main point of my critique of Habermas's rejection of revolution has to do with how this rejection affects his political theory and his theory of law, morality, and politics. I believe that Habermas risks being unable ever to recognize radical democratic agency if and when it emerges because he has already excluded its very possibility. Most importantly, belief in the possibility of a radical alternative to the existing capitalistic order identifies the legal regulations of global markets and global communication as the most important object for critical analysis. Such an analysis has a significant democratic potential if used by political agents whose subjectivity is limited by the unjust distribution of economic and discursive resources.

Critical legal positivism, as I understand it, should recognize the fundamental importance of the category of social revolution. Unjust social regulations can be destroyed and new ones can be created. Although a longing for radical changes of this kind often includes the belief that political efforts to bring about revolution should be final,[21] for instance, should create a definitely just society—revolution itself does not have to be understood in this way. Politics as a democratic practice of both social cooperation and struggle can never be finalized, but unjust social orders marked by the exploitation of humans and nature under capitalism, patriarchy, or racism can be radically challenged by alternative projects of social organization.

This means that both legal rules and legal systems should be subjected to moral critique. Most importantly, legal orders that are currently not exposed as human-made legal orders should be scrutinized. The legal regulation of wealth production has global impact even though it is in most cases the result of a purely democratic process, if any. Either these regulations do not claim moral legitimacy, and therefore radically deviate from modern law, or they somehow presuppose such legitimacy without offering an opportunity to challenge it. In both cases, critical legal positivism can assist democratic agents by exposing the positivity of legal regulations of economic relationships.

## JUSTICE AND CRITICAL ETHICS

If I am right, and social positions are crucial in order to make injustice appear as precisely injustice, what is the function of ethics? How should studies of morality be conducted? My answer to these questions is that the ethicist should serve progressive political agency in three ways. First, her theory can counteract different forms of normative legitimization of conventional regulations. Second, her theory can assist and encourage the reflexive articulation of progressive normative positions. Third, her theory can choose not to recognize any progressive normative position as morally true or definitive.

Ethics, philosophical as well as theological, should be a critical enterprise. Ethicists seek to offer instruments for resistance to various kinds of ideological projects that legitimize injustice or make it invisible. In order to perform this task, the ethicist focuses on scrutinizing social structures and relationships, not personal morality.[22] Ethics, when critical, is thus a form of ideology critique that uncovers social injustice rather than offering personal strategies to accept unjust structures or adapt to them.

A critical ethicist does not distance herself from the particularity of injustice, be it contextual or dependent on different social positions in society. Her theory is neither supported nor falsified by means of ideal cases constructed to illustrate moral intuitions of *the* philosopher. Instead, she tests her theory through analysis and critique of the normative dimensions of actual practices and structures.

In this respect, Hart was right to use utilitarianism's capacity to uncover the democratic deficit in European societies after the Second World War as an argument in favor of utilitarian normative theory. However, the critical potential of utilitarian position is limited by the same feature of utilitarianism that historically made it politically potent, namely its normative individualism. In the utilitarian assessment of a normative position, individual preferences, interests, or well-being are fundamental. The actual interests of individuals replace the metaphysical teleology of natural law theory, making utilitarian ethics a democratic enterprise. However, this same individualistic reduction of the moral perspective—methodological, its proponents describe it—in fact reduces morality to how it appears to individuals.[23] As I have demonstrated in my critique of Hart and Raz, such a reduction makes ethics compatible with many forms of social injustice, among which inequality is the most important one.

A related feature of utilitarianism in its various forms is its focus on the total of wellbeing rather than the just distribution of wealth, resources, and power. In looking for a critical model for social ethics, I am therefore moving in another direction and defending a constructivist account of deontological ethics.

This account should be sensitive to new political agencies that challenge existing institutions and conventional regulations—legal and moral in our case. Ethics with a significant critical potential has its point of departure in those instances where conventional regulations appear as unjust—and they do it for those who *experience* domination, exploitation, violence, and other forms of social injustice.

"Assisting the reformer" is a difficult task, however. I have already problematized Hart's liberal understanding of a progressive political agency that utilitarian ethics and Hartian legal positivism aspire to serve. However, even alternative perspectives of progressive political agency are facing serious challenges. To begin with, those subjected to exploitation, domination, and other forms of social injustice are also included in the ideological legitimization of particular forms of injustice. Women in patriarchal societies tend to embrace conventional norms as legitimate and are often hostile to those—women and men—who are critical of patriarchal ideology. Many representatives of the working class in contemporary Europe regard poor migrants from other countries, rather than agents with economic power, as responsible for deteriorating social conditions. Obviously, experiences of injustice do not automatically transcend the ideological legitimization of a particular social order. This means that the ethicist who wishes to serve a progressive political agency must involve herself in a critique of ideology, even when such an ideology is embraced by the oppressed.[24]

Moreover, while a consolidated progressive agency[25] may seem obvious in its immediate context, it is always ambivalent by virtue of being marked by existing social structures. The subjectivity of any progressive agent preserves elements of the unjust order that such subjectivity seeks to reform, which is why "post" in post-colonialism or post-apartheid contexts indicates a dialectics of negation and continuity.

Additionally, ethics should not be reduced to the advocacy of alternative positions on morality and positive legislation. Even when we have strong arguments in support of the progressive character of a particular agency—such as the negation of patriarchy, colonialism, or racism—the ethicist should not become a mere propagandist for political programs. In this particular regard, I am critical of those political cynics on the left who severely underestimate the need for reflexivity on behalf of liberation movements.[26] Such a reflexivity does not allow the ethicist who supports a particular form of resistance to regard her theory as pure instrumental to an already consolidated political agency.

It is of course possible, and in many cases justified, for a theorist to argue in favor of a particular political project, such as Rawls's political liberalism. However, I agree with Jürgen Habermas that the ideational construction of more just social structures is a democratic rather than a speculative theoretical enterprise. Politics is never about the implementation of morality, be it religious morality, liberal theory of justice, or human rights. Therefore, a critical ethicist resists political moralism when it presents itself as a trans-political theory of social justice.

My perspective on critical ethics involves a rejection of the very possibility of a normative judgment as true or definite. This is so because both conventional and critical morality are dependent on material conditions—conditions that cannot be transcended by ideational efforts. This is not to say that ideals and ideal-driven practices are mere superstructures of material social relations. Rather, ideational practices should be seen as dialectically tied to material structures. Materiality here mostly means the economic and social conditions that are pre-assigned to people of a particular generation and society. Those conditions are constantly changing due to different factors, including ideational, but they cannot be chosen through an entirely volitional act.

The dialectic of normatively driven volition and the materiality of human existence does not negate the project of moral phenomenology, at least not entirely. For many reasons, it is valuable to offer philosophical, that is, highly abstract, transcriptions of moral responsibility from the first-person perspective (as, for example, in Kant and Levinas) or communicative rationality (Habermas, Alexy, and Benhabib). However, such a phenomenology always contains a risk of what Michael Goodhart defines as "categorical normativity." Categorical normativity, as used by Goodhart, downplays the social contingency of normative commitments while simultaneously establishing "authoritativeness" on the justificatory level of abstract morality.[27]

I find the critique issued by Goodhart (directed mostly against Forst, Fraser, and Bohman) relevant. Goodhart is right to insist that a Kantian[28] democrat should demonstrate how her theory resists political moralism and normative closure. Let me therefore offer a defense of a particular Kantian ethics that is democratic by virtue of its critical potential with regard to the social structures of contemporary capitalism in general and the legal regulations of these structures in particular.

## OPEN UNIVERSALISM AND EQUALITY

When looking for the instruments of a critique of the moral quality of legislative practices and legal regulations, it is preferable to adopt a deontological ethical model that regards the principle of equal respect for human dignity as the main test of justified normativity. As noted earlier, this is not to say that such a normative ethical model is true. Nor am I claiming that utilitarianism can be proven false. However, if our aim is to offer a normative ethical theory with a significant critical potential that is compatible with legal positivism, we should look in a deontological direction.

Let me elaborate on a position that places the principle of equal respect for human dignity in the center of deontological ethics. To begin, we must keep in mind that the Kantian principle is not *a description* of the dignified life. In virtue ethics, for example, dignity signifies a particular way of life—a life with dignity, a life worth being called human. Such a dignity is a virtue cultivated by individuals. Obviously, even under the most pressing conditions many people act with great dignity. Some would say that difficult social conditions in many cases promote a deep personal solidarity with others and hence the humanity of moral agents. I do not question this in regard to personal morality and moral phenomenology.[29] However, here our concern with human dignity derives from the perspective of a social ethics that can contribute to moral critique of law and hence a critique of social structures. As the Muslim proverb has it: "God leaves the house when poverty enters it." The saying does not mean that poor people cannot live a life of dignity. The idea is that those in power who sustain unjust relations and force people into poverty are responsible for creating inhuman conditions, for de-humanizing people, even when those people manage to sustain dignity as part of their personality.

Thus, the principle of equal respect for human dignity should be understood as entirely practical; its function is to guide human actions, not to *describe* a humanity that deserves particular respect or protection. The principle is egalitarian in that it demands equal respect for humanity of each and every one regardless their "moral worth." This becomes most obvious in the human rights project—human rights are legitimate claims toward states on behalf of every human being and these rights need not been "deserved" by people.

In my view, both Kant himself and many Kantians after him smuggle metaphysical elements into the moral principle of respect for human dignity when presenting the faculty of reason as the most valuable marker of humanity to be respected. However, nothing prevents a critical Kantian from further "purifying" the second formulation of the categorical imperative by regarding it as entirely practical. This means that the principle should not assume any particular description of human nature. The categorical principle, which states that we should always *act* as to *treat* humanity in each and every person as an end, must be formal in relation to descriptions of what the humanity to be respected *is*.[30]

This understanding of the categorical imperative has two highly relevant normative implications. The first is the meaning of "categorical." The categorical demand to respect human dignity is independent of how people actually behave. For example, descriptive political realism can inform our analysis of society and human behavior by pointing to the fact that individuals and collectives typically act on egoistic motives. However, this does not imply that institutions based on unrestricted individual or collective egoism are morally justified.

The second implication is an acknowledgment that humanity, as well as inhumanity, appears differently in various contexts and from different social positions. Therefore, practical reason can only prescriptively *reclaim* the categorical moral principle in each particular situation. Racism, patriarchy, poverty, misrecognition, and exploitation are all examples of structures that bring about experiences of violation of human dignity. However, these structures are concrete and different. They vary between contexts and therefore give rise to particular experiences of injustice. As Raz rightly argues, a moral critique of legal regulations must be a critique of particular social relationships that these regulations sustain. On this view, we need the practical knowledge—that is, knowledge from participatory perspectives—of particular social structures in order to demonstrate when and how positive law legitimizes violations of human dignity.

I therefore propose a deontological normative theory that opens up the principle of equal respect for each and every person's humanity, leaving the question of *how* human dignity should be respected to particular practical discourses. In this regard, I agree with Michael Walzer's argument that we should reframe universality claims in such a way that the particular experiences of actual human beings are not devalued from the perspective of the universalist.[31] Walzer, who calls his version of universalism "reiterative universalism," uses resources from the Jewish tradition in order to understand the dynamics of the universal and the particular. As he writes:

> Just as we are capable of recognizing a particular history as our own and another history as someone else's, and both of them as human histories, so we are capable of recognizing a particular understanding of autonomy and attachment as our own and another understanding as someone else's, and both of them as moral understandings. We can see the family resemblances and acknowledge at the same time the particular character of each member of the family. The acknowledgment is additive and inductive, as I suggested earlier, and so it does not require an external standpoint or a universal perspective (from which we might leap immediately to a covering law). We stand where we are and learn from our encounters with other people. What we learn is that we have no special standing; the claims that we make they make too, the children of Israel and the children of the Ethiopians. But it is a moral act to recognize otherness in this way.[32]

Although Walzer is here focusing on cultural experiences of otherness and recognition, it is plausible to assume that social differences also present us with particular perspectives of crucial importance for moral judgment. To view the otherness of a social minority and its equal right to moral judgment in the way proposed by Walzer means recognizing our shared humanity without longing for either submission or assimilation.

Hence, the defining feature of the categorical principle of respect for human dignity is its openness to particular forms of injustice. At the same time, the egalitarian character of the principle is preserved by the suggested model of universalism. To respect humanity in each and every person, or, in a negative form, to reject violations of human dignity legitimized by conventional social hierarchies between persons and groups, is an egalitarian version of a universal moral principle that does not demand the uniformity of implementation.[33] Most importantly, such a principle offers a moral justification of political struggle on behalf of those who experience social structures and conditions as unjust.

Why, then, do we need the principle of human dignity in the first place? Could not we just say that the normative claim to equality between humans does the entire job of morally justifying social relationships and institutions?

In my view, there are two key reasons to defend the principle of equal respect for human dignity. The first is that even when we agree that inequality cannot be morally justified, we tend to disagree about the types of inequality that should be regarded as fundamental.[34] In contemporary social ethics, the moral dimension of equality is often reduced to a distributive paradigm of liberal justice. This is obvious in the liberal discourse on human rights. Human rights are understood as commodities that the state offers (or should offer) to individuals and, in some cases, minorities. Even progressive liberal interpretations of human rights, such as those of Rawls and Dworkin, reduce the political agency of citizens by presenting them as the recipients of rights and freedoms distributed by the state. As several critics have shown,[35] distributive models of equality—liberal and otherwise—do not cover all significant forms of social injustice.

The categorical principle of equal respect for human dignity, on the other hand, is not identical with any particular model for equality, for instance, an egalitarian theory of justice. Rather, it is an instrument for the context-sensitive scrutiny of different dimensions of justice. Sometimes, the demand for redistribution of economic resources and power is the most plausible interpretation of the principle of human dignity. In other situations, misrepresentation and misrecognition appear as violations of humanity. The lack of freedom and relevant forms of power is yet another form of inequality as injustice. In her three-dimensional approach to justice, Nancy Fraser uses this insight when claiming that a radical-democratic interpretation of the principle of human worth includes distribution, recognition, and political representation.[36] By means of feminist critical theory, she reconstructs different forms of social injustices in the contemporary world.

Human dignity, as Fraser understands it, is violated when humans are prevented from participating "as peers in social life."[37] This move to equal participation is an *interpretation* of the principle of equal moral worth through particular social experiences of injustices in a particular time. Framing the demand for equality as a demand for the respecting of human dignity means inviting the underprivileged to make their particular experiences of injustice an issue for moral-political discussion.

This is not the same as claiming that the actual preferences of persons and groups are the only legitimate source of moral justification of social regulations. Utilitarian models of equality, though historically progressive, offer a limited version of both justice and democracy if compared with the model I am defending here. Utilitarians are right when they claim that moral arguments in the context of democratic practices are connected to and limited by material factors. Naturally, these arguments are combined with different types of bargaining and tactical approaches. However, in contrast to utilitarian ethics, which tends to identify justice with an aggregation of the factual interests and preferences of people and therefore always asks minorities to adjust their expectations, deontological ethics does not compromise the moral claim to equality.

A deontological model that places the principle of equal respect for human dignity at the heart of social ethics allows us to interpret human rights and democracy as interdependent. In the chapter on Habermas, I argued in favor of his dialectical understanding of human rights and democracy because this understanding keeps rights political and democracy human. Political and legal strategies for counteracting concrete forms of inequality may differ, but, as Habermas puts it, the character of principle of equal respect for human dignity remains *constitutional* for any legitimate model of democracy.

Constitutionalism is here a model for legitimate power and stipulates that those whose dignity is violated have a fundamental right to question social regulations in all forms, including legal. On this account, democratic constitutionalism is not only an instrument for the preservation of a particular form of democracy. Rather, it is the model for a political and social organization that secures the possibility of social transformations driven by the unprivileged.

The second reason in favor of the principle of human dignity as fundamental to egalitarian critical ethics has to do with the unfortunate fact that people do not agree that embracing equality is the defining feature of any genuinely moral position. Even in modern societies, where human rights and democracy have become significant elements of collective self-images, many would argue that both human rights and democracy can be justified in terms of a minimal level of protection (or participation) of individuals and groups.[38] On this view, human rights and democracy are compatible with social inequality.

Hopefully, the underprivileged can utilize the principle of respect for each and everyone's humanity in order to demonstrate that particular forms of inequality violate their dignity, that is, dehumanize them. If I am right, the desire for social equality can be justified morally and legitimized democratically when it is related to concrete experiences of de-humanization. Although material privileges tend to make us less sensitive to injustices that disproportionately affect the underprivileged, resources for social solidarity exist. A society in which violations of human dignity of persons and groups are normalized is not a good society for anyone, or so the classical narratives of various traditions claim. The democratic challenge is thus to identify and utilize contextual resources in order to demonstrate *how* concrete forms of social inequality constitute violations of human dignity.

## HUMAN DIGNITY, POLITICS, AND LAW

Deontological ethics, which I have argued supports and further strengthens the critical potential of legal positivism, gives prominence to the categorical principle of respect for each and everyone's humanity. What exactly the principle means in any concrete situation is essentially open to interpretation. Interpretations are related to social positions and material factors such as the structure of a society, market, or public discourse. However, these factors are not "objective" if objectivity is understood as agent-independency. People are dependent on social structures, but collective human agency can either sustain them or replace them with new structures.

How, then, should a critical legal positivist[39] use the principle of equal respect for human dignity if her aim is to improve the moral quality of law? In my view, there are four key trajectories: ordinary legal practice guided by the constitutional protection of human rights; constitutional judicial review; strategic litigation; and the democratic critique of law.

To begin with, the principle of respect for human dignity can be *posited* as an interpretative key within ordinary legal practice. As Ronald Dworkin has argued, this principle helps the judiciary to interpret legal regulations in a coherent way. For Dworkin, as for many other proponents of the principle, this coherence is dependent on the state "taking human rights seriously." The legitimate exercise of power, including litigation, should thus be guided by a constitutional promise to treat all persons with equal respect and concern.

In practice, this means that some level of power analysis is introduced into legal reasoning. For example, if human rights are understood as a constitutional trump that individuals and minorities can use in order to restrict the power of majority, the judge should dare to interpret social positions of importance for her cases in such a way that a lack of power (social and economic power included) indicates a stronger responsibility on behalf of the state. Ronald Dworkin uses this argument to justify reverse discrimination (affirmative action) in the United States. On the constitutional level, he asserted the priority of the right to be treated as an equal over the right to equal treatment. In the context of adjudication, such a priority demands a contextualized analysis of the situations of different agents such as applicants to prestigious educational programs. Candidates such as Afro-Americans who are exposed to structural discrimination are reasonably entitled to affirmative action on behalf of the state.[40]

In a similar manner, power analysis can be utilized when other hard cases are decided upon, such as restrictions of the right to free speech, the right that Dworkin himself regards as nearly absolute. As I have argued elsewhere, restrictions of the right to free speech are justified when they are necessary for protecting vulnerable minorities from racism.[41]

Dworkin himself believed that his interpretative theory of law undermined legal positivism altogether by giving prominence to the moral principle of equal respect and concern. As noted earlier, I believe he was wrong. His theory contradicts a legal positivism that depicts legal reasoning as pure (a-moral) implementation of politically posited regulations. However, Hart has already pointed out that legal systems often incorporate moral norms and principles. It is up to the legislator to give legal force to moral norms. This means that if we jettison Dworkin's idea of objective normative truths accessible to the judge—as I believe we should—his interpretative theory can be combined with both descriptive political realism and legal positivism.

There is no doubt that the moral principle of human dignity is often violated by legally valid norms. But this principle—when it is constitutional and "taken seriously"—has great potential to preserve the link between ordinary legal practice and scrutiny of the moral quality of law. Whenever legal practice is expected to be bound by the constitutional protection of equal human dignity, ordinary litigation can contribute to the improvement of the moral quality of law.

Another related usage of the principle of equal respect for human dignity are the different forms of constitutional judicial review. The normative appeal of the procedure of judicial review is fundamentally bound up with the idea of constitutional democracy. As Christopher Zurn puts it in his illuminating analysis of democratic constitutionalism: "[various types of] institutions of constitutional review [. . .] should, in general, be oriented toward broadening democratic participation, increasing the quality of political deliberation, and ensuring that decision making is reasons-responsive and thereby democratically accountable."[42] In Zurn's view, the institutions of judicial review should be formed as an element of constitutionalism in deliberative democracy.[43] Independent judicial or quasi-judicial bodies perform a significant function in a democracy if and when they act as guardians of fundamental principles for will formation and the exercise of power.

While admitting that human dignity should be a constitutional moral principle to apply within legal practice as well as in judicial constitutional review, I do not believe that we can expect the moral quality of law to be sustained by legal practices in the strict sense. The development of human rights law, like the limitations of that law, illustrates this point. Human rights law has made sufficient progress in many countries, but it would be naïve to expect socially privileged lawyers to see the egalitarian principle of human dignity as crucial to justified legal judgment.

Some legally recognized instruments are, however, accessible for those who seek to enforce the principle of human dignity as foundational within the legal sphere. Strategic litigation is one such instrument. While it can take different forms, it always seeks to connect judicial practice to political morality. This is clearly expressed by Francine Morris:

> Strategic litigation is a method used to select suitable cases ("test cases") to bring to court in order to achieve a specific outcome. The intention is that these legal proceedings will have a positive broader impact on law and policy development as well as setting a precedent for the outcome in similar cases. The objectives of strategic litigation can be intra-legal and extra-legal. Intra-legal objectives concern the interpretation, application and content of the law in question, for example establishing whether certain treatment is direct or indirect discrimination. Extra-legal aims do not target the content of the law in this way, but instead typically serve to raise awareness and/or put pressure on relevant actors to take measures to prevent discrimination. This may be done by for example attracting media attention to shed light on a particular problem, sector, or group.[44]

The principle of equal respect for human dignity is central to the strategic litigation conducted by lawyers for European equality bodies. It is expected to guide the interpretation of legal regulations. However, such an interpretation alone cannot guarantee the moral quality of law.

Furthermore, the legal possibilities for preserving and developing the moral quality of law (interpreted in light of the principle of equal human dignity) can be restricted by political power. For example, it is easy to restrict the practice of strategic litigation by simply reducing funding for equality bodies. This is also true in relation to the judicial bodies that make constitutional reviews. Consider the following Swedish case of judicial review. In the Constitution of Sweden (The Instrument of Government, Chapter 8), it is stipulated that "[t]here shall be a Council on Legislation [the opinion of which] shall be obtained before the Riksdag takes a decision" on a number of fundamental matters, including human rights, rule of law, or environmental issues. The opinions of the Council are expected to be taken very seriously, for instance, incorporated into the deliberation in the government and the parliament (*Riksdag*). Due to the normalization of populism in Sweden, this practice has recently been weakened such that legislators now tend to disregard the Council's opinions.

Moreover, historical experiences indicate that when a non-democratic or even repressive political regime is about to be established, legal cultures tend to adjust to new regulations and either ignore constitutional principles of moral nature or "reinterpret" their meaning.

Thus, the moral critique of law in light of the principle of equal respect for human dignity (including some forms of constitutional review) is a political enterprise. Although politicians are most often cynical about the demand for moral justification, the moral principle becomes an instrument for critique through political agency of those dissatisfied with the status quo. In a materialist interpretation of the relationship between moral justification and politics, it is up to the underprivileged to revitalize the moral dimensions of the political by demonstrating the injustice of their particular position and demanding social justice.

Social injustice when experienced as such drives political agency and becomes an active force for democratic politics. In this regard, I agree with Habermas's dialectical approach to rights and democracy, which views the critique of the moral quality of the law as *constitutional* to a genuine democracy. As highlighted earlier, "constitutional" in this context is not reduced to a written constitution awaiting correct interpretation by a supreme court. Rather, it is the ongoing democratic constitution of a particular society, which claims or reaffirms its basic principles by means of democratic deliberation.

When Christopher Zurn argues in favor of a critical theory of the constitutional review, he also uses the Habermasian understanding of democracy

Within the deliberative paradigm of democracy constitutional review is political, it

> scrutinizes the reason justifying statutes, regulations and governmental actions, insuring both the public autonomy and private autonomy rights necessary for procedural legitimacy, and ensuring the nondistorted character of the "official" circulation of power from the communicative power of the weak public sphere, to the legislative and then administrative and judicial power of the strong public sphere.[45]

In a deliberative democracy, the moral principle of equal respect for human dignity can and should be used as critical in regard to both political and legal power. In contrast to the later Habermas, I argue that democratic constitutionalism, if it is to remain democratic, must include the possibility of a radical change of social structures (including property and wealth accumulation). Although social development should not be understood as linear progress, there are always possibilities to change existing social structures.

In order to uncover and utilize such possibilities, democratic constitutionalism stipulates that citizens are equally entitled to respect because they are the source of the legitimate exercise of power. If interpreted in a non-metaphysical manner, the moral political principle of respect for human dignity is identical with recognition of each person's equal democratic status. When people argue that they are marginalized, exploited, or suppressed within a particular social order protected by law, or when they demand changes, they are acting as democratic subjects. Democratic societies should recognize this as a constitutive element of the sociality and counteract the temptation to suppress critics in order to preserve the status quo.

Importantly, recognition of democratic political subjectivity should not be conditioned by majoritarian status. The constitutional principle of equal respect for human dignity stipulates that various minorities should have equal opportunity to defend their position in public and expect a significant impact on politics and legislation. In this regard, the protection of rights of minorities is vital for any functional democracy. Raz is right in claiming that all individuals should be guaranteed the possibility of making real-life choices, that is, of having access to traditions. Moreover, the constitutional recognition of minority rights is crucial for sustaining pluralism as fundamental for democratic cultures. When European anti-Islamic racists argue that Islam and Muslims threaten democratic institutions, they are in practice defending a democracy whose institutions promote homogeneity and conformism.

Obviously, the principle of human dignity included in a written constitution[46] does not in itself guarantee the democratic constitutionalism that is characterized by endorsement of both private and public autonomy. However, it seems to inspire some political agents and trouble others. Those political agents whose aim is to frame democracy as a regime of unrestricted power of ethnic, religious, or some other kind of majority regard the principle of human dignity as an illegitimate moralistic limiting of democratic power. When the nationalist party Sweden Democrats gained access to political power in the 2022 election,[47] they immediately announced their intention of abolishing the anti-discrimination law. The idea that the state has a constitutional duty to respect the humanity of all individuals contradicts those nationalistic models of social relationships that expect minorities to accept assimilation, subordination, and other forms of injustice.

Another important element of constitutional democratic culture that becomes obvious in light of the principle of equal respect for human dignity is the fundamental right of citizens to question the boundaries of politics. Consider, for example, the current tendency to present the regulating of economic relationships (from banking to taxations) as apolitical. This can be done if one understands economic relationships either as impossible to regulate or as the object for regulatory *techniques* rather than politics. The technocratic reduction of the scope of the political restricts in practice the democratic agency of citizens, especially those who are disadvantaged within particular capitalistic regimes. This restriction must be challenged, and the principle of human dignity justifies such a challenge. When economic injustice is experienced and publicly described as dehumanization, the moral quality of the legal regulation of markets becomes a democratic issue.

In my view, this insight still includes the potential for a radical social transformation, which explains why many political agents on the right prefer to ally with nationalists and thereby jeopardize democracy altogether rather than admit that economic inequality is a legitimate matter for democratic debate.

To conclude, the principle of equal respect for human dignity is crucial to a deontological ethical model that has significant critical potential in relation to social conventions, even if it is not a form of natural law theory. The proponent of this kind of deontological ethics views critical morality as a dimension of human relationships and collective agency. This, however, does not exclude the possibility of progressive social developments being driven, at least partly, by moral ideas and rational deliberation. The improvement of moral quality of legal systems is the most important objective for such developments.

## NOTES

1. This discrepancy is obvious in the parallel reports made by European minorities' organizations to *The United Nations' Committee on the Elimination of Racial Discrimination*.

2. I define racism as a particular legitimization of social inequality. Different forms of racism, such as anti-Islamic racism in contemporary Europe, are attempts to justify the unequal treatment of people on the basis of their culture, religion, ethnicity, etc.

3. Emilios Christodoulidis, *The Redress of Law* (Cambridge, UK: Cambridge University Press, 2021), 119–148.

4. What kinds of social groups that are in the current stage of globalization have the potential for collective political agency is one of the most important issues for both political theorizing and democratic activism. See, for example, Håkan Thörn, "Revolution as a Politics of Time-Space: From Enlightenment Modernity to Advanced Globality," in *Future(s) of the Revolution and the Reformation*, ed. Elena Namli (London: Palgrave Macmillan, 2019), 65–95.

5. It is, of course, possible for an observer to realize that regulations that do not bind her agency are binding law for others. This is, however, a deficient perspective for the student of law.

6. Robert Alexy, *A Theory of Legal Argumentation. The Theory of Rational Discourse as Theory of Legal Justification* (Oxford, UK: Oxford University Press, 2009).

7. Unless we firmly disconnect the legal and the democratic dimension of modern law which happens when legal positivism marked by positivistic epistemology becomes an operational ideal for legal practice. Ronald Dworkin offers a convincing critique of such a positivism. See Ronald Dworkin, *Justice in Robes* (Cambridge, MA: Harvard University Press, 2006).

8. For a highly illuminating interpretation of this Marxian insight, see Brian Leiter, "Marx, Ideology, Legal Positivism," *Virginia Law Review* 101, no. 4 (2005): 1179–1196.

9. One could say that most lawyers profit from social injustice and therefore do not recognize them as injustice. There are of course cases of social solidarity when members of (out)groups support disadvantage groups in their efforts to uncover and oppose injustice. However, as several theorists point out, such an (out)groups' solidarity is demanding and includes significant risks of imposing their own agenda on ingroup members. See Andrea Sangiovanni, *Solidarity. Nature, Grounds, and Value* (Manchester, UK: Manchester University Press, 2023), 58–60. Members of (out) groups who have own experience of practices of solidarity—from different forms of feminism to anti-apartheid—testify of the profound challenge of "colonialization" of the emancipatory project of the unprivileged. See Chandra Talpade Mohanty, *Feminism Without Borders. Decolonizing Theory, Practicing Solidarity* (Durham, NC: Duke University Press, 2003).

10. Rainer Forst's argumentation in favor of the fundamental and equal right to justification can be interpreted as such an effort. It is fundamentally unjust, he claims, to limit people's opportunities for publicly questioning the legitimacy of moral norms related to the exercise of power and distributive issues. I see no good reason for excluding discussions of values. It is equally reasonable to publicly question if and how values established in a particular community (i.e., ethics in Forst's terminology) are justified.

11. Duncan Kennedy, *A Critique of Adjudication* (Cambridge: Harvard University Press, 1997), 157–179. There are, of course, different institutional solutions for the legal and political components of democratic constitutionalism. For a thorough analysis of various forms of institutional design of the constitutionalism, see Christopher Zurn, *Deliberative Democracy and the Institution of Judicial Review* (Cambridge, UK: Cambridge University Press, 2009).

12. Elena Namli, *Human Rights as Ethics, Politics, and Law* (Uppsala: Acta Universitatis Upsaliensis, 2014), 25–27.

13. Dworkin, *Justice in Robes*, 2, 58–61.

14. In this particular context, I am referring to lawyers within a single legal system. For obvious reasons, lawyers, like all of us, are more inclined to pose critical questions to social regulations in societies that differ from our own.

15. Kennedy, *A Critique of Adjudication*, 157–179.

16. There is a significant literature on the experience of social solidarity within different kinds of liberation movements. See, for example, Sebastian Garbe, *Weaving Solidarity. Decolonial Perspectives on Transnational Advocacy of and with the Mapuche* (New York: Columbia University Press, 2022).

17. One recent and still under-studied example of such an anarchy is the privatization of the state property following the collapse of the Soviet Union. The dramatic democratic deficit in contemporary Russia is obviously related to the population's experience of how economic greed and moral cynicism of "new Russians" was efficiently framed as a form of democratic emancipation. Especially interesting is that the post-Soviet legislation on property issues was enforced in technocratic terms, for instance, as something needing to be done in order to create the preconditions for democracy and effected almost entirely without democratic scrutiny.

18. Habermas's major work on politics and religion—*Between Naturalism and Religion* (Cambridge, UK: Polity Press, 2008)—is the most obvious example of his lack of attentiveness to *different* forms of contemporary religious agency within the political.

19. Boris Kapustin, "What May Be Wrong with the "End" in the End-of-Revolution Thesis?" in *Future(s) of the Revolution and the Reformation* ed. Elena Namli (London: Palgrave Macmillan, 2019), 121–152.

20. Michael Löwy, *The Theory of Revolution in the Young Marx* (Chicago: Haymarket Books, 2003).

21. John Dunn, "Revolution as a Political Category," in *Future(s) of the Revolution and the Reformation* ed. Elena Namli (London: Palgrave Macmillan, 2019), 21–37.

22. As already stated, the most important weakness of virtue ethics is precisely its focus on the personal morality and personal character of the moral agent.

23. One example of this kind of reduction is Helen Frowe's work on the ethics of war. In several publications, she argues that a reasonable position on just war can be constructed from the perspective of individual moral agency. See Helen Frowe, *Defensive Killing* (Oxford, UK: Oxford University Press, 2014).

24. The most complex and inspiring depictions of the critical democratic engagement and its challenges have been made by writers such as Maxim Gorky and P. O.

Enquist, who devote themselves to particular forms of social liberation. In Gorky's *Mother* and Enquist's *Traces in the Ocean of Stillness,* we encounter protagonists who, though working class, endorse the dominant social hierarchy. However, such endorsements can be challenged and the subjugated can develop social and political subjectivity of their own.

25. An agency already opposed to ideological legitimization of the status quo.

26. For example, Chantal Mouffe in her defense of the left populism.

27. Michael Goodhart, *Injustice: Political Theory for the Real World* (Oxford, UK: Oxford University Press, 2018), 164–165.

28. In this particular context, the Kantian signifies a philosophical position that is phenomenological on a fundamental level. Morality is understood as a phenomenon whose general and formal structure can be grasped philosophically.

29. For an analysis of radical responsibility from the first-person perspective, see, for example, Elena Namli, "*The Brothers Karamazov* and the theology of suffering," *Studies of East European Thought* 74 (2022): 19–36.

30. Many Kantians claim that some assumptions about respecting humanity are needed when the principle is justified. As a normative principle, the principle of human dignity is formal, but it must be justified with the help of some kind of assumption about "the essence" of humanity. Rainer Forst's right to justification, like other forms of Kantian rationalism, incorporates such anthropological assumptions. I believe that we should rather move in the direction suggested by Habermas, who has made a significant effort to present the justification of moral judgments as a model for communicative, i.e. social, reasoning rather than as a model for arguments that are coherent with some fundamentally human features.

31. Michael Walzer, *Nation and Universe. The Tanner Lectures on Human Values* (Oxford, 1989), walzer90.pdf (utah.edu)

32. Ibid., 527.

33. For example, such uniformity, or rather the desire for it, is easily used to transform human rights discourse into an ideology of domination. See Elena Namli, "Universal Consensus Re-examined. Critique of a Liberal Defense of the Universality of Human Rights," in Namli, *Human Rights as Ethics, Politics, and Law*, 35–62.

34. My argument here differs from Andrea Sangiovanni's argument about the link between equality and human rights. He starts by addressing "those, like us, who already affirm a commitment to moral equality, but are unsure regarding its foundations." I am less concerned about the *foundations* of equality, which I interpret as a purely normative principle. This prescriptivism is key to my version of Kantian ethics. See Andrea Sangiovanni, *Humanity without Dignity. Moral Equality, Respect, and Human Rights* (Cambridge, UK: Harvard University Press, 2017), 9.

35. Iris Marion Young's seminal monograph *Justice and the Politics of Difference* (1990) is one of the most influential contributions to the critique of distributive justice.

36. Nancy Fraser, *Scales of Justice. Reimagining Political Space in a Globalizing World* (New York: Columbia University Press, 2009), 16–17.

37. Ibid., 16.

38. See, for example, Michael Ignatieff, *Human Rights as Politics and Idolatry* (Princeton, NJ: Princeton University Press, 2001).

39. We need to bear in mind that such positivists can be either practitioners or theorists, or both.

40. Ronald Dworkin, "Reverse Discrimination," in Dworkin, *Taking Rights Seriously*, 22–239

41. Elena Namli, "Freedom of Speech—a Colonial Saint in the Catalogue of Rights," in Namli, *Human Rights as Ethics, Politics, and Law*, 119–146.

42. Christopher Zurn, *Deliberative Democracy and the Institution of Judicial Review* (Cambridge, UK: Cambridge University Press, 2009), 2.

43. Zurn is critical—rightly, in my view—of the tendency of political theorists as well as legal scholars to identify democratic constitutionalism with "constitutionalism and judicial review as carried out in the United States' system." Ibid., 8–26.

44. Francine Morris, "What is Strategic Litigation?" in *Strategic Litigation. An Equinet Handbook.* Equinet European network of equality bodies 2017, 9.

45. Zurn, *Deliberative Democracy and the Institution of Judicial Review*, 255–256.

46. I am not arguing that common law does not allow the principle of human dignity to acquire constitutional status.

47. Although not included in the government, the policies of the Sweden Democrats have been implemented by the right-wing coalition's government. The Tidö Agreement (*Tidöavtalet*) stipulates the conditions for the support given to the government by the Sweden Democrats.

# Bibliography

Alexy, Robert. *A Theory of Legal Argumentation. The Theory of Rational Discourse as Theory of Legal Justification*. Oxford, UK: Oxford University Press, 2009.

Baxter, Hugh. *Habermas: The Discourse Theory of Law and Democracy*. Redwood City CA: Stanford University Press, 2011.

Berger, Johannes. "Die Versprachlichung des Sakralen und die Entsprachlichung der Ökonomie." *Zeitschrift für Soziologie* 11, no. 4 (1982): 353–365.

Besson, Samantha and Tasioulas, John. *The Philosophy of International Law*. Oxford, UK: Oxford University Press, 2010.

Borradori, Giovanna. *Philosophy in a Time of Terror. Dialogues with Jürgen Habermas and Jacques Derrida*. Chicago: The University of Chicago Press, 2003.

Christodoulidis, Emilios. *The Redress of Law*. Cambridge: Cambridge University Press, 2021.

Dunn, John. *Modern Revolutions. An Introduction to the Analysis of a Political Phenomenon*. Cambridge, UK: Cambridge University Press, 1994.

Dunn, John. "Revolution as a Political Category." In *Future(s) of the Revolution and the Reformation*, edited by Elena Namli, 21–37. London: Palgrave Macmillan, 2019.

Dworkin, Ronald. *Freedom's Law. The Moral Reading of the American Constitution*. Cambridge, MA: Harvard University Press, 1996.

Dworkin, Ronald. *Justice in Robes*. Cambridge, MA: Harvard University Press, 2006.

Dworkin, Ronald. *Taking Rights Seriously*. Cambridge, MA: Harvard University Press, 1977.

Dyzenhaus, David. *Legality and Legitimacy*. Oxford, UK: Oxford University Press, 1997.

European Network of Equality Bodies. *Strategic Litigation Handbook*. Equinet, 2017. Strategic Litigation Handbook – Equinet (equineteurope.org).

Finnis, John. "H. L. A. Hart: A Twentieth-Century Oxford Political Philosopher." *The American Journal of Jurisprudence* 54, 2009: 25–53.

Finnis, John. *Natural Law and Natural Rights*. Second Edition. Oxford, UK: Oxford University Press, 2011.

Forst, Rainer. *Justification and Critique*. Cambridge, UK: Polity, 2014.

Fraser, Nancy. *Scales of Justice. Reimagining Political Space in a Globalizing World*. New York: Columbia University Press, 2009.

Frowe, Helen. *Defensive Killing*. Oxford, UK: Oxford University Press, 2014.

Fuller, Lon L. *The Morality of Law*. Revised edition. New Haven, CT: Yale University Press, 1969.

Garbe, Sebastian. *Weaving Solidarity. Decolonial Perspectives on Transnational Advocacy of and with the Mapuche*. New York: Columbia University Press, 2022.

Gaus, Daniel. "Rational Reconstruction as a Method of Political Theory between Social Critique and Empirical Political Science." *Constellations* 20, no. 4 (2013): 553–570.

Goodhart, Michael. *Injustice: Political Theory for the Real World*. Oxford, UK: Oxford University Press, 2018.

Grenholm, Carl-Henric. *Kritisk politisk etik. Om moralens betydelse inom politiken* (Critical Political Ethics. On Morality in Politics). Uppsala: Acta Universitatis Upsaliensis, 2024.

Habermas, Jürgen. *Autonomy and Solidarity*. London: Verso, 1986.

Habermas, Jürgen. *Between Facts and Norms. Contributions to a Discourse Theory of Law and Democracy*. Cambridge, UK: Polity Press, 1996.

Habermas, Jürgen. "Concluding Remarks." In *Habermas and the Public Sphere*, edited by Craig Calhoun, 462–480. Cambridge, MA: The MIT Press, 1992.

Habermas, Jürgen. "Fundamentalism and Terror." In *Philosophy in a Time of Terror. Dialogues with Jürgen Habermas and Jacques Derrida*, edited by Giovanna Borradori, 25–81. Chicago: The University of Chicago Press, 2003.

Habermas, Jürgen. "Human Dignity and the Realistic Utopia of Human Rights." *Metaphilosophy* 41, no. 4 (2010): 464–480.

Habermas, Jürgen. *Justification and Application*. Cambridge, UK: Polity Press, 1993.

Habermas, Jürgen. *The Lure of Technocracy*. Cambridge, UK: Polity, 2015.

Habermas, Jürgen. *Moral Consciousness and Communicative Action*. Cambridge, UK: Polity Press, 1990.

Habermas, Jürgen. *Theory and Practice*. London: Heinemann Educational Books, 1974.

Hare, Richard M. *Moral Thinking. Its Levels, Method and Point*. Oxford, UK: Clarendon Press, 1981.

Hart, H. L. A: *Essays on Bentham. Jurisprudence and Political Theory*. Oxford, UK: Oxford University Press, 1982.

Hart, H. L. A. *Essays in Jurisprudence and Philosophy*. Oxford, UK: Clarendon Press, 1983.

Hart, H. L. A. *Law, Liberty, and Morality*. Stanford, CA: Stanford University Press, 1963.

Hart, H. L. A. "Positivism and the Separation of Law and Morals," *Harvard Law Review* 71, no. 4 (1958): 593–629.

Hart, H. L. A. *The Concept of Law*. Third edition. Oxford, UK: Oxford University Press, 2012.
Heller, Hermann. "Authoritarian Liberalism?" *European Law Journal* 21, no. 3 (2015): 295–301.
Hägerström, Axel. *Inquiries into the Nature of Law and Morals*. Stockholm: Almqvist och Wiksell, 1953.
Hägerström, Axel. *Social teleologi i marxismen* (Social Teleology in Marxism). Uppsala: Akademiska Bokhandeln, 1909.
Hägerström, Axel. *Socialfilosofiska uppsatser*. Stockholm: Bonniers, 1966.
Ignatieff, Michael. *Human Rights as Politics and Idolatry*. Princeton, NJ: Princeton University Press, 2001.
Kamali, Mohammad Hashim. *Shari'ah Law. An Introduction*. Oxford, UK: One-world, 2008.
Kapustin, Boris. "What may be wrong with the 'end' in the end-of-revolution thesis?" In *Future(s) of the Revolution and the Reformation,* edited by Elena Namli, 121–152. London: Palgrave Macmillan, 2019.
Kelsen, Hans. *General Theory of Law and State*. Clark, NJ: The Lawbook Exchange, Ltd, 2009.
Kelsen, Hans. *Pure Theory of Law*. Clark, NJ: The Lawbook Exchange, Ltd, 2002.
Kennedy, Duncan. *A Critique of Adjudication*. Cambridge, MA: Harvard University Press, 1997.
Laborde, Cécile. *Critical Republicanism*. Oxford, UK: Oxford University Press, 2008.
Laudani, Raffaele, ed. *Secret Reports on Nazi Germany. The Frankfurt School Contribution to the War Effort*. Princeton, NJ: Princeton University Press, 2013.
Leiter, Brian. "Marx, Law, Ideology, Legal Positivism." *Virginia Law Review* 101, no. 4 (2005), 1179–1196.
Licari, Francois-Xavier. *An Introduction to Jewish Law*. Cambridge, UK: Cambridge University Press, 2019.
Löwy, Michael. *The Theory of Revolution in the Young Marx*. Chicago: Haymarket Books, 2003.
MacCormick, Neil. *H. L. Hart*. Second Edition. Stanford, CA: Stanford Law Books, 2008.
Marmor, Andrei. "Holism, and Interpretation: The Epistemic Foundations of Dworkin's Legal Theory." *Law and Philosophy* 10, no. 4 (1991): 383–412.
Menke, Christoph. *Critique of Rights*. Cambridge, UK: Polity, 2020.
Mohanty, Chandra Talpade. *Feminism Without Borders. Decolonizing Theory, Practicing Solidarity*. Durham, NC: Duke University Press, 2003.
Morris, Francine. "What is Strategic Litigation?" In *Strategic Litigation Handbook*. edited by Francine Morris, Julia DeMarinis Gidding, and Tamás Kádár, Equinet, 2017.
Muller, Ingo. *Hitler's Justice. The Courts of the Third Reich*. Cambridge, MA: Harvard University Press, 1991.
Murphy, Liam. "The Political Question of the Concept of Law." In *Hart's Postscript: Essays on the Postscript to 'The Concept of Law'*, edited by Jules L. Coleman, 371–409. Oxford, UK: Oxford University Press, 2001.

Namli, Elena. "*The Brothers Karamazov* and the Theology of Suffering." *Studies of East European Thought* 74 (January 2022): 19–36. https://doi.org/10.1007/s11212-021-09454-x

Namli, Elena. "Christianity and Human Rights Law. Orthodox Perspectives." In *Christianity and International Law. An Introduction*, edited by Pamela Slotte and John D. Haskell, 317–336. Cambridge, MA: Cambridge University Press, 2021.

Namli, Elena. *Human Rights as Ethics, Politics, and Law*. Uppsala: Acta Universitatis Upsaliensis, 2014.

Persson, Madelene. *Frågan om människovärde. En kritisk studie av mänskliga rättigheter i rasismens och migrationens tidevarv*. Uppsala: Acta Universitatis Upsaliensis, 2020.

Pettit, Philip. "The Basic Liberties." In *The Legacy of H.L.A. Hart: Legal, Political, and Moral Philosophy*, edited by Matthew Kramer, Claire Grant, Ben Colburn, and Antony Hatzistavrou, 201–222. Oxford, UK: Oxford University Press, 2008.

Piketty, Thomas. *Capital in the 21st Century*. Cambridge, MA: Harvard University Press, 2014.

Pistor, Katharina. *The Code of Capital. How the Law Creates Wealth and Inequality*. Princeton, NJ: Princeton University Press, 2019.

Porter, Jean. *Ministers of the Law. A Natural Law Theory of Legal Authority*. Cambridge, UK: William B. Eerdmans Publishing Company, 2010.

Porter, Jean. *Nature as Reason. A Thomistic Theory of the Natural Law*. Cambridge, UK: William B. Eerdmans Publishing Company, 2005.

Rahmatian, Andreas. *Credit and Creed: A Critical Legal Theory of Money*. London: Routledge, 2019.

Rajagopal, Balakrishnan. *International Law from Bellow. Development, Social Movements and Third World Resistance*. Cambridge, UK: Cambridge University Press, 2003.

Rawls, John. *A Theory of Justice*. Oxford, UK: Oxford University Press, 1972.

Rawls, John. *Political Liberalism*. Expanded edition. New York: Columbia University Press, 1993.

Raz, Joseph. *The Authority of Law*. Second edition. Oxford, UK: Oxford University Press, 2009.

Raz, Joseph. *Between Authority and Interpretation. On the Theory of Law and Practical Reason*. Oxford, UK: Oxford University Press, 2009.

Raz, Joseph. "Disagreement in Politics." *American Journal of Jurisprudence* 43, no.1 (1998): 25–52.

Raz, Joseph. *Engaging Reason. On the Theory of Value and Action*. Oxford, UK: Oxford University Press, 1999.

Raz, Joseph. *The Morality of Freedom*. Oxford, UK: Oxford Scholarship Online 2003 (1988).

Raz, Joseph. *Practical Reason and Norms*. Oxford, UK: Oxford University Press, 1975.

Sangiovanni, Andrea. *Humanity without Dignity. Moral Equality, Respect, and Human Rights*. Cambridge, MA: Harvard University Press, 2017.

Sangiovanni, Andrea. *Solidarity: Nature, Grounds, and Value*. Manchester, UK: Manchester University Press, 2023.

Schauer, Frederick. "Legal Positivism and the Contingent Autonomy of Law." In *Judicial Power, Democracy and Legal Positivism*, edited by Tom D. Campbell and Jeffrey Goldsworthy, 215–228. New York: Routledge, 2000.

Scheuermann, William E. "Capitalism, Law, and Social Criticism." *Constellations* 20, no. 4 (2013): 571–586.

Schweiker, William. *Theological Ethics and Global Dynamics*. Hoboken, NJ: Wiley-Blackwell, 2004.

Shoikhedbrod, Igor. "Revolution or legality? Confronting the Spectre of Marx in Habermas's Legal Philosophy." *Contemporary Political Theory* 20, no. 1 (2020): 72–95.

Spaak, Torben. "Kelsen's Metaethics." *Ratio Juris* 35, no. 2 (2022): 158–190.

Torben Spaak and Patricia Mindus, eds. *Cambridge Companion to Legal Positivism*. Cambridge, UK: Cambridge University Press, 2021.

Spång, Mikael. *Emancipation, Democracy and Modern Critique of Law. Reconsidering Habermas*. London: Palgrave Macmillan, 2018.

Stout, Jeffrey. *Democracy and Tradition*. Princeton, NJ: Princeton University Press, 2004.

Swaminathan, Shivprasad. "Projectivism and the Metaethical Foundations of the Normativity of Law." *Jurisprudence* 7, no. 2 (2016): 231–266.

Thörn, Håkan. "Revolution as a Politics of Time-Space. From Enlightenment Modernity to Advanced Globality." In *Future(s) of the Revolution and the Reformation*, edited by Elena Namli, 65–96. London: Palgrave Macmillan, 2019.

Tuori, Kaarlo. *Critical Legal Positivism*. Milton Park, UK: Taylor and Francis, 2002.

Vattimo, Gianni. *Nihilism and Emancipation. Ethics, Politics, and Law*. New York: Columbia University Press, 2007.

Walzer, Michael. *Nation and Universe. The Tanner Lectures on Human Values*. Oxford, 1989. walzer90.pdf (utah.edu).

Walzer, Michael. *The Paradox of Liberation*. New Haven, CT: Yale University Press, 2017.

Wilkinson, Michael. "Authoritarian Liberalism in the European Constitutional Imagination. Second Time as Farce?" *European Law Journal* 21, no. 3 (2015): 313–339.

Young, Iris Marion. *Justice and the Politics of Difference*. Princeton, NJ: Princeton University Press, 1990.

Zurn, Christopher. *Deliberative Democracy and the Institution of Judicial Review*. Cambridge, UK: Cambridge University Press, 2009.

# Index


adjudication, 19, 37, 38, 42, 53, 109, 110, 130, 131, 144
affirmative action, 144
Alexy, Robert, 126
anarchism, 55
anti-discrimination law, 124, 148
Aristotelian ethics, 24, 82, 94
assimilation, 148
Austin, John, 51, 53, 54
authority, 21, 32, 73, 78–80, 108, 126–28; legal, 21, 89; legitimate, 73, 78, 79, 86; morally justified, 79; social, 79
autonomy, 22, 44, 79–84, 99, 101, 108, 114

Bentham, Jeremy, 54, 57, 60, 61, 67

capitalism, 19, 22, 23, 97, 98, 116–19, 124, 134–36, 139
capitalist markets, 112, 118, 130
coercion, 63, 64, 66, 126
cognitivism, 6–7, 19, 29–31, 33, 39–42, 45, 58, 59, 131
collective agency, 87
collective rights, 88
communicative reason, 104, 111
communitarianism, 83, 85–87
conformism, 147
constitutional, 19, 103, 107–10, 113–15, 118, 124, 130, 142, 144–48
constitutionalism, 53, 104, 143, 145, 147
constructivism, 39, 46, 63; ethical, 16, 22, 50, 119, 130; social, 12, 14, 16, 24, 25, 30, 41, 49, 61, 67, 119, 130, 131
conventions, 93; moral, 12–14, 22, 54, 77, 81, 83; social, 46, 60, 83
cooperation: social, 78, 80, 82, 84–90, 92, 98, 104
critical ethics, 136, 138, 143
critical morality. *See* morality, critical
critical theory, 8, 21, 97, 106, 114, 119, 124, 132, 142, 146

democracy, 15, 64, 103, 112, 113, 115, 118, 119, 135, 143, 148; aggregative, 113; constitutional, 39, 100, 101, 103, 145; deliberative, 98, 105, 113, 145, 147; liberal, 17, 42, 63, 118; modern, 99, 100, 106, 111–13, 119; radical, 23; Western, 119
democratic constitutionalism, 99, 101, 115, 119
democratic deficit, 97, 98
democratic principle, 104–6
deontological ethics, 38, 54, 59, 65, 137, 139, 142, 143, 148

dialectical understanding of law, 8, 22, 98–101, 106, 115
discourse ethics, 17, 24, 102, 105
discourse principle, 100–02, 104–05
discourse theory, 9–10, 22, 98
discrimination, 13, 66, 88, 93, 124, 130, 144
domination, 15, 63–65, 93, 128, 132
Dunn, John, 117
duties, 34, 103, 112, 129
Dworkin, Ronald, 19, 36–42, 53, 58, 59, 62, 81, 108–10, 126, 130, 140, 144
Dyzenhaus, David, 8, 15

economic relations, 125, 148
egalitarian, 38, 58, 66, 81, 116, 130, 131, 139, 140, 143, 145
emancipation, 22, 99, 114
emotivism, 44, 76
Enlightenment, 99
epistemology of law, 124–26
equality, 37, 58, 64, 107, 116, 133, 140, 142–43, 146
equal treatment, 38
ethical theory, 26n6, 39, 75, 76, 128
ethics, 11–12, 136–38
exclusionary reasons, 74, 75
exploitation, 66, 93, 132, 136, 140
expressivism, 76
external preferences, 40, 41, 48n44, 59

facticity of the law, 98, 100, 111, 119
feminist, 43, 114, 142
Finnis, John, 35, 61, 62
Forst, Rainer, 108, 139
Fraser, Nancy, 139, 142
freedom, 18, 58, 63, 64, 66, 81, 82, 86, 91, 99, 110, 114–16, 134
Fuller, Lon L., 19, 34–36

Goodhart, Michael, 138–39
Grenholm, Carl-Henric, 4–5

Habermas, Jürgen, 5, 8, 10, 17–19, 22, 97–119, 134–35, 142
Hägerström, Axel, 43–45
hard case, 53, 109, 131, 144
Hare, Richard M., 45, 46, 76, 92
Hart, Herbert L. A., 4, 5, 7–8, 17–20, 35, 40, 49–68, 103, 112–13, 134
Heller, Hermann, 15–16
historical materialism, 43
human dignity, 37, 106–07, 111, 129, 139, 142–43, 145; respect for, 36, 93, 103, 107–08, 129–30, 133, 139–48
human nature, 31, 32, 123, 140
human rights, 11, 36–38, 59, 66, 89, 93, 94, 102–04, 106–09, 115, 123, 129, 140, 143–44

idealism, 43, 104, 115, 123–24
ideology, 81, 93, 95n37, 127–28, 137
imperialism, 62, 68
individualism, 81, 82, 86, 90, 112, 137
inequality, 25, 63, 64, 84, 87, 107, 116, 128, 137, 140, 143
injustice, 24–25, 33, 38, 55, 83, 91–92, 97, 125, 128–29, 134, 136–37, 140, 148
internal morality of law, 19, 34, 35
International Covenant on Civil and Political Rights, 66
interpretative theory of law, 19, 37–39, 41, 53, 109, 131, 144
Islamophobia, 2, 11

Judaism and law, 30, 46n4
justice, 44, 115, 128, 141–42; distributive, 84, 87; social, 66, 74, 83, 87–89, 91–92, 138

Kant, Immanuel, 84, 104, 140
Kantian, 84, 85, 116
Kelsen, Hans, 29, 30, 51, 75–76, 123

law: international, 63, 64, 89; municipal, 50, 64, 67; positive, 5–9, 22, 45, 55; traditional, 9
legality, 22, 34–36
legal philosophy, 98

legal point of view, 74, 75
legal positivism, 3–7, 16–17, 22, 24, 42–43, 49–51, 108, 110, 123–25; classical, 123; critical, 126, 127, 133, 135; descriptive, 6; soft, 20
legal practice, 10, 36, 130, 131, 143–45
legal system, 35, 51, 74, 90, 126, 130, 136
legal validity, 2–4, 17, 21, 43, 51–52, 73, 75–76, 78, 90, 108, 124, 133
legislation, 37, 102, 103, 110
liberalism, 18, 21, 81, 86–87; authoritarian, 15; classical, 17; economic, 15; egalitarian, 8, 37; political, 16, 98
Luhmann, Niklas, 105

marginalization, 66
Marmor, Andrei, 39
Marx, Karl, 38, 43–44, 60–61, 100, 114, 135
Marxism, 43–44, 114
metaethics, 24, 26n6, 45, 76
Mill, John Stuart, 54, 67
Mindus, Patricia, 6–7
modernity, 99, 102, 116, 117, 119, 135
morality, 11–12, 35, 55, 83, 105, 137; conventional, 11–12, 14, 20, 23, 52, 54, 124, 127, 133, 138; critical, 7, 11–12, 14–15, 20, 22–23, 52, 54–55, 59, 62–63, 67, 90–91, 124, 127–28, 133, 138, 148; individual, 12; personal, 11, 136; political, 42; private, 14, 17, 64; social, 24, 40, 83, 85; universal, 14, 59, 92
moral critique of law, 4, 8, 15–16, 20, 49, 73–74, 86, 89, 112, 127–28, 133, 146
moral judgment, 45, 67, 76, 92, 141
moral justification, 2, 4, 30, 40, 86, 103, 124–25, 140, 142, 146
moral point of view, 97, 98
moral quality of law, 4, 17, 38, 43, 84, 87, 100, 110, 115, 127–28, 130, 132–33, 145–46
moral realism, 6–7, 37, 39, 40, 45, 60, 62
moral reason, 77, 78, 116
moral rights, 37, 40–42, 57–59, 61, 63, 66–67
moral values, 68
Morgenthau, Hans J., 5
Murphy, Liam, 62

natural law, 3–4, 9, 14, 17, 19, 23, 29–36, 60, 63, 93, 108, 111, 123
natural morality, 32, 36, 37, 43, 127, 128
Niebuhr, Reinhold, 5
non-cognitivism, 39, 45, 58, 76
normative ethics, 84, 128
normativity, 75, 98, 114; justified, 75, 76, 78; legal, 75, 77, 80; moral, 78; social, 75, 77–78
Nozick, Robert, 58

operational moral theory, 74

paternalism, 103
patriarchy, 15, 88, 93, 114, 136, 138, 140
Platonic, 100
Platonism, 103, 104, 123
pluralism, 30, 33, 56, 59, 62, 63, 147
political cynicism, 4, 123, 125, 128
political liberalism. *See* liberalism, political
political moralism, 4–5, 21, 40, 84, 91, 138
political realism, 4–5, 20–21, 132, 140, 144
politics, 4, 42, 138
populism, 146
Porter, Jean, 19, 31–33
positivity of law, 2, 6–7, 20, 98–100, 119
post-colonialism, 119, 138
power, 124, 128, 144; discursive, 124, 125; economic, 124, 125; legitimate, 143; political, 127; social, 124, 125

practical reason, 76, 77, 104, 111, 116, 140
prescriptivism, 45, 76
primary rules of obligation, 51, 52
public sphere, 22, 105, 113, 134

quietism, 55, 62, 86

racism, 11, 12, 15, 25, 66, 91, 93, 124, 128, 132, 136, 138, 140, 144, 149n2
Radbruch, Gustav, 55, 56
Rawls, John, 16, 21, 37, 58, 84, 91, 104, 115, 140
Raz, Joseph, 5–6, 17–19, 21, 73–94, 112–13, 134
relativism, 30, 33
republican, 113
revolution, 23, 25, 66–67, 87, 116–17, 133–36
right-based normative theory, 67
rule of law, 35, 36, 113, 133
rule of recognition, 51–53

sanctions, 51, 126, 127
Schmitt, Carl, 4–5, 15, 99, 115
Schweiker, William, 31
self-legislation, 99, 108, 113
separation thesis, 8, 20, 39, 50, 94, 124–26
service conception, 79, 90
sexism, 91, 132
Shoikhedbrod, Igor, 117
social class, 43
social contract theory, 104, 115
social legitimacy, 90
social reality, 12, 15, 45
sovereignty, 89, 99, 100, 118
Spaak, Torben, 6–7
strategic litigation, 13, 145–46
subjective rights, 106, 107
Swaminathan, Shivprasad, 76

teleology, 137
true propositions of law, 58, 109–10
Tuori, Kaarlo, 8–10

universalism, 25, 68, 93, 140, 141; normative, 85; open, 139–43; reiterative, 140
universalizability, 14, 46, 77, 85, 92, 93
universalization, 102, 104, 106, 111
utilitarianism, 8, 24, 49–50, 54–57, 59–61, 65–66, 68, 84, 137

value nihilism, 5, 16, 20, 25, 44–45
value objectivism, 69n23
value ontology, 19, 30, 33, 45
virtues, 82, 139

Walzer, Michael, 140, 141
will-formation, 101–03
Williams, Bernard, 84

Zurn, Christopher, 145–46

# About the Author

**Elena Namli** is a professor of ethics at Uppsala University, Sweden. Her research focuses on social and political ethics with a particular emphasis on the critical studies of human rights. She has published on philosophical as well as theological ethics. Her books include *Human Rights as Ethics, Politics, and Law* (2014), *Future(s) of the Revolution and the Reformation* (editor, 2019), and *Etik* (*Ethics*, with Carl-Henric Grenholm, 2019). Elena Namli served as a president of *Societas Ethica* from 2020 to 2024. She is editor in chief of *De Ethica*—a journal of philosophical, theological, and applied ethics.

www.ingramcontent.com/pod-product-compliance
Ingram Content Group UK Ltd.
Pitfield, Milton Keynes, MK11 3LW, UK
UKHW020209290926
15470UKWH00001B/80

9 781666 973402